CAUTIONARY NOTICE TO READERS - DISCLAIMER

Issues related to your Estate Plan are changing regularly. Regulations related to family law, wills, incapacity and other issues are always under discussion and in a state of change. Financial, tax, corporate succession, risk management strategies, et cetera. are regularly changing. The author(s), publishers and/or vendors are not providing certified advice. It is recommended that you reference relevant legislation, regulations and tax conventions in your jurisdiction. It is recommended that you seek the professional help of a Certified Financial Planner (CFP), accountant and/or estate lawyer before completing your estate plan documents.

ISBN: 978-0994783622

Published by Paul Lambe

This project is the sole work of **Paul Lambe CFP FMA**

All efforts were made to make this a proprietary work from past experience, knowledge and research in the **'public domain'.**

Public domain refers to creative works and intellectual property to which there are no property rights due to expiration, forfeiture, or not being applicable.

Please contact us by email at estategta@gmail.com.

ABOUT THE AUTHOR

Paul Lambe is a currently a Fee-For-Service Certified Financial Planner in St. John's, NL and Ontario, Canada, providing Financial Planning and Estate Management Services.

Paul spent ~20 years in Ontario, Canada as a Certified Financial Planner, serving the Greater Toronto Area.

Paul completed the following educational programs related to finance:

- Certified Financial Planner (CFP) designation in 2000.

- Financial Management Advisor (FMA) program in 2002.

- LUAC- Life and Disability Insurance Level II Licence in 1999 and held this until 2012.

- Post Graduate Marketing Management Honours- Investment Securities Profile, Humber College, Ontario 1992.

- Business and Economics studies Memorial University, St. John's, Newfoundland 1982-1987

Paul has worked as a Financial Planner since 1996, with several large financial services companies in Canada, providing advice and wealth management services to meet the financial goals and needs of clients.

Paul was a self-employed financial and estate consultant for executors, trustees and POAs from 2012-2015 and returned to this business in 2018.

Paul climbed Mt. Kilimanjaro, Tanzania in 2004 to raise funds and awareness for ALS.

Paul accomplished 'A Mountain for Maddie' in 2008, climbing Mt. Elbrus, to help fund Free the Children initiatives of Maddison 'Maddie' Babineau. Maddie passed at 15 while raising funds to build a well in an African village, for which she gave her Children's Wish to build a school.

Paul enjoys reading/research/writing, playing soccer, playing golf, mountain climbing, hiking, travel, culture and history.

TABLE OF CONTENTS

INTRODUCTION

Estate Planning is the process of arranging your personal affairs. It involves the transfer and management of assets when a person dies, becomes disabled or incapacitated, or chooses to have someone else manage their affairs.

I have spent most of the last twenty-five years working closely with clients and other professionals in the financial planning industry, especially on client's estate planning. I assisted clients in settling estates with and without estate plans in place, and can tell you it is much easier on everyone with an estate plan in place.

It is believed in industry circles that as many as 50% of the adult population do not have an estate plan in place. Some of the reasons for this are; people find the topic morbid, people not wanting to engage a lawyer and/or other professionals, or the cost and time that needs to be put into it.

It is because of this I discovered the need for The Estate Plan Workbook and How to Write your own Will - Guide and Workbook. Tools you can work on yourself at your own pace, fill in your specific details, let your wishes be known and get them down on paper.

You will establish your wishes to be included in your Will by understanding the top clauses that many Wills use, and then choosing those that are right for you.

The hardest part for most people is to make these decisions and get them on paper or some other medium. You can have a Certified Financial Planner review these decisions, and then a lawyer if you so choose. I will repeat the need to consider professionals many times in this book.

This book is a tool, workbook and a guide to help you get your wishes on paper and write your Will. Our objective is to keep it as simple as possible for the average person to understand the aspects of a Will.

This book does not give legal or tax advice but merely points out important issues in these areas. After completing this workbook, you can decide to finish your Will yourself, or use a lawyer who should be able to complete drafting your documents with relative ease, saving you money on legal fees, versus going through a complete estate planning process.

It is said that 'Estate Planning is The Process of Living and Dying Neatly'. Besides creating a descriptive Will through your estate planning, your affairs while you are alive also need to be eventually addressed, and then legal documents can be created for this purpose.

Our objective in this workbook is to help you pull together your wishes and choices for your Will at this point in time, by using common clauses.

You may realize through this process that there are gaps, complex situations or certain issues related to your Will that you may need to take care of with the help of professionals; a Certified Financial Planner, an accountant, and/or an estate lawyer.

In your Will you may need to address; your executor, guardians of minors, trusts, gifting, tax planning, beneficiary designations, joint ownership, corporate succession issues, funeral arrangements, organ donation, and risk management.

We will explain many common clauses in a Will so you get a basic understanding of the various parts. You can then go to a section at the back to fill in your wishes and notes. This is a workbook, so feel free to write in handwritten notes, checkmarks, question marks, etc., in any section that you can go back to later.

It is advisable to read the full book first then go through the workbook section, and refer back to the table of contents and reread sections that apply to you. I have purposely not included an index or a glossary to keep the workbook simple, and to recommend you reread sections completely when necessary.

How to Write your Own Will! Guide and Workbook is not a complete Estate Planning Guide, it is an introduction to writing a Will. It is for single people, the young family, couples, people with investment assets, insurance, a home and personal property who wish to get their Will completed.

We will discuss common strategies and concepts in Estate Planning, however it is outside the scope of this book to provide detailed estate planning. You should work with your Certified Financial Planner, accountant and/or lawyer on complex estate planning issues that involve more complicated trusts, business assets, blended families, more than one real estate property, substantial investment assets, and assets in multiple jurisdictions.

My objective is to also provide information relevant in most common law jurisdictions. Common law jurisdictions include those where many of the laws are from precedents, previous legal decisions usually made by a judge, court or tribunal. Common law jurisdictions include Canada (ex Quebec), UK, US (ex Louisiana), et cetera.

I personally believe that the effort I have put into this workbook will help many people get their Wills completed.

All efforts were made to make this a proprietary work from past experience, knowledge and research in the 'public domain'. Public domain refers to creative works and intellectual property to which there are no property rights due to expiration, forfeiture, or not being applicable. The law is always in the public domain, whether it consists of government statutes, ordinances, regulations, or judicial decisions.

Paul Lambe CFP FMA, 2019

I.

PROBATE AND ADMINISTRATION OF AN ESTATE

Probate is a process used to confirm the validity of a Will and the appointment of the executor, estate trustee or personal representative to act on behalf of the deceased or the estate. The executor/estate trustee can use the resulting authority given in this document(s) to settle the estate and transfer property to the named beneficiaries of the estate.

Probate and the administration of an estate are usually much easier when a deceased person has completed a detailed legal Will.

If there is no Will, there is no executor named, there is no alternate named when the executor named is deceased or unwilling to act, the executor dies in the process, the next of kin can apply for letters of administration which will confirm the legal authority of the applicant as the administrator to act on behalf of the estate and distribute property to next of kin. If no one applies, a government department usually can act as administrator.

The process of probate requires filling out forms and submitting them to the appropriate body in your jurisdiction, usually a court which then issues letters probate, letters of administration, letters of authority, letters testamentary, a certificate of executor or estate trustee, et cetera. These give legal authority to the applicant to deal with the administration of the estate through third parties such as financial institutions, government institutions, bill payees, and any entity that may require a grant of probate.

In most jurisdictions (i.e. state, provincial) the government provides access to rules and forms and you can research how the process works. Completing the probate process individually is possible for most people, however, it can be challenging at times especially with more complex assets, structures or wishes of the deceased.

Small estates, which can be defined differently in many jurisdictions, can often be settled without probate.

Probate is often required when assets are held individually, for example a savings account – the financial institution will often freeze the account when advised of the death of the owner and probate may then be required to access the funds.

- Many financial institutions allow certain payments from these accounts such as payment directly to a funeral home.
- Sole ownership of a property may also require probate.
- Probate can be required when there is no named beneficiary on assets, such as registered assets and life insurance proceeds.
- Probate can be required when there is a wrongful-death proceedings or minor dependents.

Probate fees, estate taxes or death taxes? Fees or 'taxes' owing can vary depending on your jurisdiction and the size of your estate. It may not be required where all transfers of assets are completed outside of the estate. Some jurisdictions have a minimum estate value before fees are charged, others charge a flat fee on the total value, i.e $15 per $1,000, or 1.5%, so on a $1 million estate, this can result in probate fees of $15,000 payable by the estate.

Methods of reducing probate fees? Probate fees can be reduced by employing some of the options below. Probate fees can be relatively small compared to income tax due on death, executor/estate trustee fees and/or legal fees.

- Changing assets or property to joint tenancy with your spouse, children, or other intended recipients can provide a direct transfer of assets and avoid fees. However, this may create problems such as loss of control over assets, capital gains on the change, or creditors or spouse of your joint owner making a claim.
- Naming beneficiaries on all investment accounts that allow a beneficiary, plus insurance policies, etc. It is best not to duplicate or change these beneficiary designations in your Will.
- Outside your Will you may be able to name secondary or alternate beneficiaries on investment accounts or plans and insurance policies, in case your primary beneficiaries predecease you or die in a common disaster with you.
- If you do not have a need for the assets, you can give or gift the property to your intended recipients prior to an estate.

It is advisable to review your estate plan with a Certified Financial Planner to discuss probate issues, and ascertain if employing these strategies are necessary or not.

II.

INTESTACY – DYING WITHOUT A WILL

Without a Will, the deceased's assets are distributed according to his or her jurisdiction's intestate succession law. The rules of intestacy are inflexible, and may not be in accordance with the deceased's wishes.

Intestacy can create many issues for your successors;

- Your spouse may not inherit everything you wish, as many jurisdictions split certain assets between spouse and children.
- Your estate may be distributed in a manner you had not wanted. Usually your next of kin would inherit according to the Table of Consanguinity which details blood relationships. (See Table of Consanguinity below.)
- A person may have to apply to the court to be appointed the administrator of your estate, or a government agency may become the administrator if no person applies.
- A person may have to apply to the court to be appointed the guardian of minor children.
- The court may appoint a guardian for children who may not be the person you may have chosen.
- Access to assets may be restricted until an administrator is named, the estate is settled or children reach the age of majority.
- A business could be left in an indeterminate state for a period of time.
- If in a second marriage you may unintentionally disinherit children altogether.
- A common-law spouse or partner may not receive what you may have intended.
- Family or children outside of wedlock may or may not receive what you intended.
- If you die without a spouse or blood relative the government may inherit.
- Someone may need to pay liabilities and file taxes. There are also tax planning opportunities with a Will that may be missed.

---

a) Table of Consanguinity

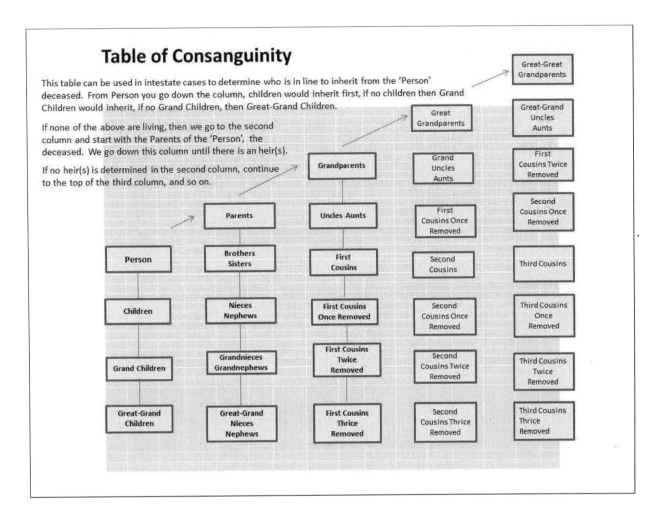

For any and all of these reasons, it is very important for you to get your wishes together, create a Will and instructions for Personal Care and Property.

III.

ESTATE PLANNING CONSIDERATIONS

There can be many other considerations and decisions for individuals and families to make outside of those already discussed such as Wills, Trusts, POAs, et cetera.

Estate Planning options are available in all jurisdictions and can be very complex if your family situation is complicated, and/or you have significant assets. We will touch on some ideas in this section.

a. Designating Beneficiaries on Qualified Accounts and Plans

Beneficiary designation can be made on most retirement accounts, registered assets, pensions, insurance policies/contracts, and trusts.

Possible reasons for beneficiary designation:
1) Easier transfer of assets
2) Avoidance of probate
3) Tax strategies, deferral or reduction

- Designating minors as beneficiaries can create problems, as the jurisdiction may hold assets in trust until the age of majority, and then the beneficiary would receive all. This may still be too young to manage considerable assets. Consider a testamentary trust in your Will for all minor beneficiaries on plans.
- Some jurisdictions have rules protecting spousal rights as a beneficiary.
- Keep beneficiary designations up to date on your accounts and plans, as the most recent designation should prevail. Be careful not to make a conflict in your Will with designated beneficiaries on accounts and plans.

b. Joint Ownership

When property is owned by two or more people it is considered jointly owned.
1) Joint Tenants - have the right of survivorship, so the assets usually pass directly to the survivors and avoid probate and estate fees or taxes. In many jurisdictions the matrimonial home is deemed a joint tenancy under legislation.
2) Tenants in Common - usually do not have the right to survivorship. So the deceased's share of the property would pass through their estate to their beneficiaries, who could become a joint owner, or the property is sold.

It is important to determine which type of joint ownership you would like and make sure details are included in the ownership agreement as some jurisdictions treat joint tenancies and tenancies in common the same.

When you have assets as joint tenants, it is highly recommended that you write your intentions for the asset. Challenges can occur if you do not communicate your intentions. I.e. For the ease of transferring assets on death, people change assets to joint tenants, with one child.

- There may be an understanding that the child will distribute the assets to other siblings. This may result in the asset having to go through probate.
- Or, the intention is for that child to receive the assets as a joint tenant.

Other children can challenge this intention if there is no indication, usually in writing, that that was the intent. There have been rulings based on what is believed to be the intent of the deceased. Therefore, write out your intentions when it comes to all joint assets.

Problems with joint ownership can include:

- Loss of control – asset(s) are managed by all owners
- Exposure to creditors of joint owners
- Triggering of capital gains
- Reporting of future income

A common alternative to joint ownership is an inter vivos trust.

c. Taxation

Taxation is very different in most jurisdictions, and if tax savings are a large part of your estate planning objectives then you will need to see a professional as it is outside the scope of this workbook. It is advisable to consult with a qualified Certified Financial Planner and accountant, who are known experts in taxation in your jurisdiction.

Some considerations for your jurisdiction(s):

1) Capital gains tax and elections
2) Spousal rollovers
3) Dependent rollovers
4) Charitable contributions
5) Trusts

Trusts for instance historically had clear tax advantages; however legislators are constantly changing the rules as they search for more tax revenue sources.

d. Life Insurance

Life insurance can be the simplest method of providing for and protecting an estate.

- If you have little or no assets and wish to provide funds for your dependents or beneficiaries. I.e., if you are single and do not have the funds to pay for your own funeral, then life insurance can be the best option. A basic life insurance policy of $100,000 can help pay for funeral expenses and have funds left over to help out surviving family members.
- If you have minor children you may need a larger policy to pay for their expenses until they reach the age of majority. You may also want to provide for their post-secondary education.
- You may want to provide for payment of the mortgage, imagine leaving your spouse as a single parent caring for children alone. If funds are not there to cover expenses they may be forced to sell the home.
- Life insurance can also be left in a life insurance trust with payments made over a period of time to named beneficiaries.

> Life Insurance trusts can be created by making the designation within the policy or plan, clearly identifying the trustee(s) and beneficiaries. I.e. To my brother _____ in trust for my children, _____, _____. The terms and powers of the trust can then be written into the Will; otherwise the trustee will be subject to jurisdictional regulations.

See your CFP, or a licensed insurance agent to discuss various options for your situation, including types of life insurance and premium options.

e. **Gifting**

Gifting or giving assets to family prior to passing can avoid possible problems for the estate and ensure the appropriate people have the assets. You can see the difference you make as they use them while you are alive. I.e. Consider a gift of money each year before a special time or event, birthday, anniversary, holiday, it can allow all to enjoy the event more.

With gifting assets such as investments or real estate, there are issues to consider like triggering capital gains, future needs, and giving up control. I.e. passing the family cottage may create a capital gain; however, future gains appreciate to the new owner. Capital losses may be able to be used through gifting of capital assets.

Making donations to charity – many charitable donations during life and after death to a charity come with tax benefits.

f. **Multiple Wills**

There are some situations where multiple Wills should be considered.
- Assets in another jurisdiction – it is often easier for an estate to be settled if there is a Will written in the jurisdiction of the property owned.

Different jurisdictions have different tax rules, probate and legal considerations. I.e., how would a property transfer or sale in Florida or the Bahamas be handled? What if there was a divorce or marriage?

In some foreign jurisdictions it can make sense to hold the property or assets in a trust with named beneficiaries for a less complicated transfer.

- Business assets and succession –you may have a separate Will to transfer the shares or ownership of a business outside of probate. Considerations related to these business interests are outside the scope of this workbook.
  1) Proprietorship – Sole owner
  2) Partnership – Share of partnership
  3) Incorporated – Share(s) of corporation
     a. Transfer the shares to family members
     b. Sell the shares to partners, shareholders, employees, or third parties
     c. Wind up the business and sell assets

g. Other Considerations with your Estate Planning

- Determine how much immediate cash may be needed to pay bills on passing. Keep it in an accessible account for the estate representative.
- Keep an updated net worth statement each year with details on your assets and liabilities.

Get your estate in order now, to ease the burden for family.

VI.

YOUR LAST WILL AND TESTAMENT

A Will, also known as a Last Will and Testament, is the cornerstone of any properly structured estate plan. Originally it is believed a Will referred to real estate assets and a testament referred to tangible personal property. The terms have and continue to be used interchangeably.

A Will or Testament is a legal document that, if properly executed declares a person's final wishes. The person who creates the Will, the testator (male) or testatrix (female), names one or more persons known as an executor/executrix, personal representative, estate trustee or liquidator to manage the distribution of the estate property to the named beneficiaries, etc., and carry out any other final wishes. A person's beneficiaries/divisees/legatees are those who are to receive the person's property.

We will use testator to refer to testator and testatrix, and executor to refer to executor/executrix, personal representative, estate trustee or liquidator in the interest of simplicity. Be mindful of what is appropriate in your jurisdiction.

Common items in a Will are: naming an executor, designating your choice of guardians of minor children, designating assets that will be held in trust, stating what age minor children will receive their inheritance, indicating how your affairs can be structured to minimize income taxes, probate fees, succession duties, inheritance taxes and if desired funeral and\or burial instructions. These are just some of the many personal choices which are addressed in the preparation of a Will.

The best time to prepare a Will is immediately. Many people neglect it for too long, others leave it until they hear of someone else's dire situation, when a domestic contract such as a cohabitation, marriage or separation agreement requires the parties to make a Will, and others before a trip or major surgery who are forced to make decisions very quickly.

You and your spouse, common-law spouse or partner should have your own Wills and should discuss and be familiar with the requirements of each other's Will. A Will can be a joint will as in a husband and wife will where the parties involved make very similar or identical provisions. These have also been known as a mirror/mutual/reciprocal wills in many jurisdictions.

Usually, any person over the age of majority in their jurisdiction and being of sound mind - testamentary capacity, can create a Will. Some jurisdictions may specify an age at which a person can create a Will, such as 17, 18, etc, instead of the age of majority. A regular member of the armed forces or a seaman may create a Will if under the age of majority.

Testamentary capacity is the most common reason used in contesting a Will. The test for a person's testamentary capacity in order to execute a valid Will or alter a Will through i.e. a codicil is similar in most jurisdictions. In most cases a testator must:

- Understand they are making a Will and that it dictates their wishes or true intentions for their property when they are deceased.
- Understand the scope of their property, size of their estate, which they are relinquishing to their beneficiaries.
- Understand the terms of the Will and what effect they will have.
- Understand who is or should be expected to inherit property under the Will, such as a spouse, children, a disabled dependent, et cetera.
- Understand who, if excluded, may be able to make a claim against the estate.
- Have no disorder of the mind that perverts their sense of right or prevents the exercise of their natural faculties in disposing of their property by Will.

If you are writing your own Will, you should give proper consideration to these points and make sure you cover them off. You may wish to see your personal physician for an assessment before executing your Will.

There is no legal requirement that a Will be drafted by a lawyer, however it is highly recommended to avoid problems, as the person will not be around to clarify. Most capable people can create a legal will without the help of a lawyer. As long as the Will meets the legal requirements of your jurisdiction, it is valid.

A lawyer should definitely be considered if there is a complex or complicated issue, such as a large estate, if there is a change in marital status, if any assets are held outside of your current jurisdiction, or if there is a question of capacity, et cetera. If you feel you can address these issues yourself with personal reading and research, you are totally entitled to do this, and accept any and all responsibility.

A properly executed Will in most jurisdictions has the testator declare to the witnesses that they are about to see him/her sign their Last Will and Testament at the end of the document, and he/she the testator then signs the document. The witnesses then sign a short declaration in the Will that they were present and witnessed the testator's signature. A good practice is for the testator to begin by initialing each page of the Will in succession, each witness initial each page with the testator, then complete with the testator's signature and witness signatures as mentioned in the appropriate areas.

There can be different requirements by jurisdiction, so be sure to verify your requirements. A few jurisdictions required three witnesses as did Georgia, Vermont and New Hampshire at one time, so old Wills may still exist. Puerto Rico required three witnesses plus a notary public. Colorado and North Dakota, allowed a testator to have a signature notarized instead of witnessed. We cannot provide the differences in all common law jurisdictions, and we want as much information to be relevant as possible in as many jurisdictions, so we will suggest which items you may need to research.

In most jurisdictions the witnesses should be <u>disinterested</u>, not a beneficiary of the Will. They can be disallowed from receiving under the Will, or they could invalidate their status as a witness. Find witnesses who will not receive anything under the Will under any circumstances, or you risk voiding certain provisions in the Will, opening it to challenge, or possibly invalidating the entire Will.

Some jurisdictions do allow nuncupative (oral) wills in certain circumstances, such as during a final illness, or military personnel on active duty. The oral wishes for these Wills may need to be written down soon after by as many as three witnesses required to be present for the oral Will. These oral Wills should only be undertaken as a last resort and under legal advisement.

Most jurisdictions recognize holographic Wills, which are handwritten by the testator. A holograph Will is completely written by hand and signed by the testator. Holographic Wills do not need to be witnessed in most jurisdictions, and can be probated with minimal requirements. It should be dated but not required.

Holographic wills can provide complications for the executor by not having enough detail or instruction. They can be appropriate where the estate is minimal or in emergency situations where someone needs to leave last minute instructions and wishes.

No legal words are required in a Will, so it can be written in plain language. Some say that many of those in the practice of law purposely make writing a Will more difficult than it needs to be by using unnecessary, incoherent and archaic language instead of plain language and that many in the practice of law fearmonger the difficulty of Will preparation.

I have noticed that there are others who support the initiative of making language in Wills more readable. The validity a Will can be challenged if someone believes the testator had a lack of understanding of the language and contents of the Will.

It can be very important to use plain language so that your intentions are as clear as possible. You can rewrite any clause or part of a clause yourself to be sure that your intent is clear.

There is no standard form to a Will, so many clauses you decide to use in the body can be in any order, however historically clauses have to flow, so there are practices that are usually followed.

Statutory Wills are another low cost, simple, basic Will available in a few jurisdictions; however, they are very narrow in scope and what you can accomplish. A statutory Will is a form that has been created by a statute. The statutory Will includes the rules under the statute, you can get a copy through an internet search, complete it, have it witnessed correctly, and you have a valid Will. These forms usually cannot be legally altered.

Other statutory Wills in some jurisdictions can be a different type of Will that is set up under a specialist court for those who lack mental capacity. These often require legal representation.

International Wills

Most rules related to Wills are very similar in most jurisdictions around the world, especially in common law jurisdictions. When people own property in more than one jurisdiction, they need to consider the possibility of multiple Wills or an international Will.

In 1973, at an international convention, many countries came together in an attempt to make Wills recognizable and enforceable across international boundaries and jurisdictions for each country which became a party to the Convention. These 'International Wills' can be valid in all jurisdictions where the convention applies. However, caution is recommended, as some countries, states and/or provinces have their own specific rule differences, especially those under civil code versus common law.

It is very important to keep in mind that if you have multiple Wills to deal with (i.e. a corporation or a property in another jurisdiction), that you be careful in wording this clause so as not to invalidate the other Will(s). It is highly recommended if you have the need for an international Will or multiple Wills to seek legal advice.

It is always your responsibility to verify the requirements in your jurisdiction, or you risk the possibility of an invalid will.

a) **Items to Prepare or Consider for Your Will.**

You should use the '**APPENDIX – PERSONAL LEGACY WORKBOOK**' to fill in all of the following related information and notes.

1. **Estate Goals**

The first step is to decide on goals for the remainder of your lifetime, and prepare for them, as well as what you want to do with your estate when you die.

You may want to:
- Leave a neat estate, with as much detail as possible so that your executor has great direction and detail, your wishes are well documented and your beneficiaries are provided for as you wish.
- Leave a suitable estate for your spouse, children or grandchildren (i.e. through life insurance?).
- Provide for a child or adult who has a physical or mental impairment (i.e. in a trust).
- Minimize or defer estate expenses and income tax.
- Transfer your business effectively to a family member or other (i.e. complex planning).
- Leave specific personal items to selected people, specific legacies or bequests (i.e. mother's ring to daughter).
- Donate to your desired charities.
- Make your funeral wishes known (i.e. burial or cremation?).
- Make your organ donation wishes known (i.e. to a university for science or specific organs only?).

2. **Personal Information**

Besides your name and address, information related to your family and also historical information should be provided.

3. **Financial Information**

Your assets and liabilities should be provided to determine the appropriate detail of your Will and possible planning opportunities.

4. Beneficiary(s)

Beneficiaries are the people or entities you name in your Will to receive a benefit from your estate or those you name on a plan, account, policy or trust. It is important to give the correct full name and relationship for each beneficiary. (i.e. Your spouse's nieces and nephews, are yours by marriage but not blood. You should indicate or elaborate on the relationship for non-blood beneficiaries, as in 'My husband, _____'s niece _____ _____.')

A residual beneficiary is a person or entity who shares in the residue of the estate after all other obligations have been met, including the payment of debts, taxes, expenses and bequests/legacies have been honored.

A testamentary trust beneficiary is a person or entity you have indicated will receive a benefit from your estate, but it will be held in a trust. A trust does not have to be a complicated entity; the simplest form of testamentary trust can be created by indicating at what ages minor children are to receive their inheritance. It is recommended that more details be given for a trust for minors indicating how funds will be paid out over time or accessed by trustees for their benefit.

It is a good idea to also name alternate or contingent beneficiaries in case the primary beneficiary(s) predeceases you, dies in a common disaster with you, cannot be found, or in rare cases declines to receive the assets.

What should you do if you believe a beneficiary may be difficult to locate? Provide any information related to this type of beneficiary; where they were last known to live, full name, relationship, last known addresses, other people to contact, occupation, education, etc.

There are heir, beneficiary, genealogy, and DNA searching and locating services available in most jurisdictions or online, so any instruction or power for your executor to engage these professionals for a period of time would be recommended in these cases, and then indicate what should happen to the assets if the beneficiary is not located.

Beneficiary designations on certain investment plans or accounts as well as insurance policies are usually done with the provider and **not** duplicated in your Will unless there is a good reason for it. Most providers of accounts make sure you fill in this information on signup or on account changes.

If you absolutely desire to name beneficiaries of registered plans or insurance policies in your Will, because they are for some reason not named on the plan with the provider, you can. It may cause assets to flow through your estate, creating possible probate fees and/or tax implications.

Promises you made to persons during your life are not binding. However, if someone performs services or lends you money in return for you leaving something in your Will, the courts have previously ruled favorably for that person.

Many jurisdictions protect the rights of a spouse and/or dependents to a share of the estate, even if they are not named as beneficiaries.

b) Common Clauses for Wills.

All Wills are different, mainly because almost all have a different testator, most have a different executor, often the beneficiaries will be different as well as the residue to be distributed.

The relatively basic clauses in this workbook may not meet the needs of a complex estate. The clauses discussed in this workbook represent the clauses that would be included in most Wills. If you search for examples of Wills, either on the internet, in law books, from probated estates, you will find that all these types of clauses are used, many will be written differently, but achieve the same or similar objectives.

The main reason for each clause is to dictate your true intention with respect to the specific clause used, so the more you include, the clearer your intentions will be. You can add in your own words, anything that clarifies your intention.

We will explain each clause and then give examples of that clause as used in a previous Wills. You can checkmark the example clause that you feel most appropriate for your circumstances. These check marked clauses can form the basis for your Will. If you feel you need to add to a clause, make notes alongside to get the most benefit from this exercise.

1. Introductory Clause/Exordium Clause

This is the first paragraph or sentence in the Will.
- It identifies the testator/testatrix and should include any variation of the person's name, or aliases used to hold property.
- It states a legal domicile - your permanent residence or intended residence in your jurisdiction, especially if you are living temporarily outside your jurisdiction.
- It can include the testator's occupation.
- It can include the date the Will is created, signed and witnessed.
- It can include a declaration of being of sound mind and body.
- It can include a declaration of not acting under duress or undue influence. Undue influence can invalidate a Will, if challenged successfully.
- It can also include revocation of any prior Wills. We will discuss this separately below.

[Example 1.1

This is the Last Will and Testament of 'First Name Middle Name Surname', of 'Permanent Residence and Jurisdiction', made this 'Date of Month' day of 'Month', 'Year'.

[Example 1.2

I, being of sound mind and body do hereby declare that this document is the Last Will and Testament of 'First Name Middle Name Surname', of 'Permanent Residence and Jurisdiction', made this 'Date of Month' day of 'Month', 'Year', 'Occupation'.

[Example 1.3

I, 'First Name Middle Name Surname', resident in the , City/Town of _____, in the Province/Territory/State of _____, in the Country of _____, being of sound mind, having sound and effective memory, not acting under duress or undue influence, and fully understanding the nature and extent of all my property and the disposition of said property, do hereby make, publish, and declare this document to be my Last Will and Testament, (From here on referred to as my Will), and do hereby revoke any and all other wills and codicils previously made by me, 'Occupation', made this _____ day of _____, _____.

Add-ons:

These add-ons can be used if the issue specifically applies to you and you want to be clearer on your intentions, such as an additional statement to the in contemplation of marriage.

If the testator is making a Will in contemplation of marriage, the introductory clause should include an additional statement to this effect.

[Example 1.4

I, 'First Name Middle Name Surname', of 'Permanent Residence and Jurisdiction', declare that this is my Last Will and Testament made in contemplation of marriage to, _____, and is intended to take effect whether or not the marriage takes place.

2. Revocation Clause

You should make a declaration to revoke all previous Wills and codicils that were created before the date of the new Will. This will clarify that your newly written, dated and properly witnessed Will is your valid Will to be followed. This declaration can avoid any possibility that a previous Will or codicil would be brought forward by someone to contest terms in the new Will.

In many jurisdictions;
- Wills are automatically revoked by a subsequent marriage.
- A Will can be revoked in many jurisdictions by operation of law due to marriage, divorce, the making of a new Will or physical destruction of the Will.

It is very important to keep in mind that if you have multiple Wills to deal with (i.e. a corporation or a property in another jurisdiction), that you be careful in wording this clause so as not to invalidate the other Will(s). It is highly recommended if you have multiple Wills to seek legal advice.

[Example 2.1

I revoke all my prior wills and codicils.

[Example 2.2

I hereby revoke all former wills , codicils and testamentary dispositions of every nature and kind made previously.

[Example 2.3

I hereby revoke all former wills and testamentary dispositions by me at any time heretofore made.

3. Defining and/or Gender Clause

A defining clause can be used to expand on terms used in your Will. For your executor, executrix, trustee, or other term you may use interchangeably or specifically to apply to several terms, when it comes to the singular/plural or masculine/feminine/neuter. He or she can be just he, him or her can be just her, executor can be executors, etc.

[Example 3.1

Words used in this my Will regardless of the gender or number specifically used, shall be deemed and construed to include any other gender, masculine, feminine or neuter, or the singular and plural as the context requires.

[Example 3.2

Unless the context otherwise clearly indicates, words used throughout this my Will includes either in the singular include the plural, the plural includes the singular, and the neuter gender includes the masculine and the feminine.

4. Appoint an Executor/Estate Representative

An estate representative can be known as an Executor/Executrix, Personal Representative, Estate Trustee, Liquidator, et cetera. in various jurisdictions and should be appointed in your Will. This person or trust will be responsible for distributing the property according to the terms of the Will. We will use executor, estate trustee, trustee or representative interchangeably to refer to these in the workbook.

It is very important to take the necessary time and consideration to choose an appropriate executor as this person will be charged with the task of carrying out your final wishes. You may appoint more than one person to act as executor, if the estate is complicated, or you prefer to have two working together to ensure wishes are carried out properly. You can indicate if they should act jointly or 'jointly and severally'.

- Joint executors often have to work together, agree and sign together.

- 'Jointly and severally" appointees can act jointly or, independently in a separate or individual way, 'decide and sign' together or individually.

By law, in most jurisdictions executors are required to act together and in agreement, therefore executors should never be appointed jointly and severally unless there is good reason. 'Jointly and severally" appointees are more commonly used in Powers of Attorney.

One thing we will never be sure of is the order of death, who can say that old will die before young? We see common disasters, illnesses, and accidents every day, we cannot be sure of the order to hold from old to younger. It is therefore a good practice to name alternates in your Will for executor, beneficiaries, trustees, guardians, in case the person(s) predeceases or cannot act for other reasons.

To make a good choice for your executor please consider the following:
  i. Choose someone you can trust.
  ii. Consider someone who is competent, has knowledge related to executorship and/or can manage with appropriate help.
  iii. The person(s) should not be someone who would have a conflict of interest.
  iv. Financially proficient, can understand and account for financial matters.
  v. Consider the persons age and health, you do not want someone who may predecease you.
  vi. Do not think that a relative is always the appropriate choice; you need someone who will look out for all beneficiaries as you will indicate, and handle pressure from beneficiaries.
  vii. Consider an executor in your jurisdiction. Executors from outside your jurisdiction may have to post bond, or there may be restrictions.
  viii. Consider naming two children if they are adults to avoid any resentment with favoring one child over the others.
  ix. Speak to your possible executor first to determine if they would be willing.
  x. Consider someone who is capable of carrying out any and all of the following tasks and possibly more:
    - Search for your Will
    - Arrange reading of the Will
    - Secure your residence, assets, documents and any other property
    - Arrange for funeral and /or burial if directed
    - Get death certificate(s)
    - Compile an inventory and a list of assets and liabilities
    - Arrange for necessary insurance continuation on assets
    - Manage business interests for immediate needs
    - Cancel subscriptions and services
    - Delete internet profiles
    - Manage digital assets
    - Arrange for probate and paperwork to be completed
    - Search for next of kin and legitimate heirs
    - Estimate taxes owing and holdback funds until confirmed
    - Advertise for creditors

- Inform government agencies and financial institutions
- Collect debts owing and pay debts owed
- Arrange for consolidation, distribution and/or sale of assets. Home and contents, cottage and contents, business, investments, bank accounts, income sources, et cetera
- Deal with insurance contracts
- Apply for death benefits
- Gather and review previous tax details and file appropriate tax returns
- Deal with estate legal matters, i.e. file lawsuits or defend against them
- Satisfy bequests and legacies
- Assure heirs and beneficiaries of proper accounting, distribution and timelines
- Get income tax clearances
- Get releases from beneficiaries

More notes on executorship:

i.   Consider letting your family know what your Will says and who you have chosen so it can limit any future arguments.

ii. Consider giving your executor a copy of your Will and estate plan in advance to help them with their obligation.

iii. An executor may need to provide a bond as security to administer your estate.

iv. If you cannot find someone you know, then consider professional help. There are options available for a professional agent to help an executor, as I do; or other options for professionals to act as your executor for compensation, i.e. lawyers or trust companies.

v.   Estate administration and liquidation can be a complex process involving a lot of research, transactions and paperwork. Each estate settlement is different in complexity. Consider the time, effort and capability required.

vi. Even if an estate is relatively straightforward, it can take between one and two years to be fully administered and distributed.

vii. Other professional services may be required such as real estate maintenance, legal, investigative or genealogical/heir research, et cetera.

Appoint an executor/estate representative clause:

[Example 4.1 (One executor)

I appoint as my executor my [relationship - husband/wife/common law spouse/son/daughter/friend/lawyer, et cetera.],_____.

[Example 4.2 (One executor)

I appoint my [relationship - husband/wife/common law spouse/son/daughter/friend/lawyer, et cetera.],
_____ to serve as the sole Executor/Executrix of this my Will, and I herein after refer to him/her as my 'Executor'.

[Example 4.3 (One executor with alternate)

I appoint my [relationship - husband/wife/common law spouse/son/daughter/friend/lawyer, et cetera.],
_____ *to serve as the sole Executor/Executrix of this my Will, and I herein after refer to him/her as my 'Executor'. If he/she is unwilling or unable to act as my Executor, I appoint my [relationship - husband/wife/common law spouse/son/daughter/friend/lawyer, et cetera.],* _____ *sole Executor of this my Will.*

[Example 4.4 (Two executors acting jointly, with alternate, with sole successor executor.)

I appoint my [relationship - husband/wife/common law spouse/son/daughter/friend/lawyer, et cetera.],
_____ *and my [relationship - husband/wife/common law spouse/son/daughter/friend/lawyer, et cetera.],* _____ *to serve as Co-Executors/Executrixes of this my Will, and I herein after refer to him/her as my 'Executor'. If either of them is unable or unwilling to serve, the remaining Executor shall continue to serve as sole successor Executor hereunder. If both of these Executors of this my Will are unwilling or unable to serve, I appoint my [relationship - husband/wife/common law spouse/son/daughter/friend/lawyer, et cetera.],* _____ *sole Executor of this my Will.*

Add-ons:

Giving one executor veto or decision making authority. (When there is more than one executor.)

[Example 4.5

I request that my trustees make every reasonable effort to make their decisions jointly and unanimously, however, in the event they are unable to do so, _____ *shall have the ultimate decision making authority.*

Exclusion of a person from acting as an executor clause.

[Example 4.6

I do not wish for [relationship - husband/wife/common law spouse, friend, et cetera.],
_____ *to serve as my Executor/Executrix or administrator under any circumstances.*

5. Waiver to Post Bond or to a Surety

To protect an estate, and executor or estate trustee may be required to post an estate administration bond, or provide a surety. A bond can be an insurance policy to protect the estate and beneficiaries from fraud or wrongdoing. A surety is usually a person who assures the executor will complete tasks as indicated by putting up assets. Bonds are often required for an executor from outside the jurisdiction of the assets. An executor may be relieved from posting a bond by adding a waiver of bond clause.

Waiver to Post Bond or to a Surety Clause

[Example 5.1

I declare that my named executor, co-executor or alternate, who is not resident in 'Jurisdiction', shall not be required to post a bond and/or security for acting as my executor.

[Example 5.2

No individual acting as an Executor under this my Will shall be required to post a bond and/or security for acting as my executor notwithstanding the laws of any country or other jurisdiction to the contrary.

Dispositive Clauses

Dispositive clauses can take up or be part of many provisions of a Will. An almost infinite amount can be written on dispositions and gifts through a Will. Clauses that address vesting, transfers, specific gifts/bequests/legacies/devises, basic to complicated trusts, administration, powers to act, etc.

We will review many of these dispositive clauses, and how they are or can be intermingled with other clauses.

Keep in mind when you choose your dispositive clauses that they do not conflict with each other. Taxes, debts, expenses, and any other obligations should be considered before you choose your clauses, and assets or cash should be retained to meet these obligations. Many times legacies, bequests and/or devises have to be delayed until taxes, debts, expenses, and any other obligations are calculated and paid. Investments or real estate may need to be sold, and the final net value of these may not be known until sold because of market conditions at the time.

6. Vesting Clause/Transfer of Property to the Executor

A vesting clause transfers and vests legal title of the assets ('property') of the deceased to the executor, and also gives the power and obligation to the executor to carry out the directions stated in the Will for the benefit of the beneficiaries. The word 'property' is the legal term which means all assets of every kind and not only real estate or investment assets.

Keep in mind that once assets have been transferred to the executor, this is considered a 'trust'. The estate of a person is essentially a trust. A trust is an arrangement whereby a person (a trustee/executor) holds property as its nominal owner for the good of one or more beneficiaries.

All statements in a Will that deal with specific assets to be given or transferred to a named beneficiary can be considered trusts. When these transfers and administration are completed, the trust is basically wound up.

Many people have the notion that all trusts are complicated entities, however, see Example 3 below, this is the creation of a nominal trust, where the executor (surviving spouse), transfers all the property of the deceased (basically residue) to him/her self, and then the estate/trust would be wound up.

These are basic trusts and we will call them Executor Trusts for this section of vesting or transfer of property to the executor. (See our **Trust** section for more detailed information on trusts.)

[Example 6.1 (Vesting/transfer of property to the executor clause)

I give all my property to my executor upon the following trusts:

[Example 6.2 (Vesting/transfer of property to the executor clause)

I give all my property of every nature and kind and wherever situate, including any property over which I may have a general power of appointment, to my said Executor upon the following trusts, namely:

[Example 6.3 (Vesting/transfer of property to the executor clause)

This clause would give all property to a spouse as beneficiary, who is also the executor. This is essentially a trust for the executor/spouse to gather all property of the deceased and facilitate the transfer to the surviving spouse (him/her self). This is a common clause in basic mirror/mutual Wills where spouses basically use the same clauses to leave everything to each other.

I give all my estate, both real and personal, of every nature and kind and where ever the property is located, including any property over which I may have a general power of appointment, to my [relationship - husband/wife], [Beneficiary name], if he/she survives me for a period of [thirty (30) days], for his/her, own use absolutely.

Executor Trusts: These clauses/trusts are created with the Vesting Clause/Transfer of property to the executor to manage the estate as a trust, as below.

Examples of specific trusts created for the executor to manage as trustee, to distribute as per directions to the specific beneficiary(s).

[Example 6.4

*I give all my property of every nature and kind wherever situate, both real
and personal and including any property over which I may have a general power of appointment, to my Executor upon the following trusts, namely:*

I give to my son_____ any and all land to which I may become entitled from the estates of my late mother and father.

[Example 6.5

*I give all my property of every nature and kind wherever situate, both real
and personal and including any property over which I may have a general power of appointment, to my Executor upon the following trusts, namely:*

I give to my common law spouse, _____ , my dwelling house and land.

[Example 6.6

*I give all my property of every nature and kind wherever situate, both real
and personal and including any property over which I may have a general power of appointment, to my Executor upon the following trusts, namely:*

If my daughter, _____ survives me by 30 days, my executor shall transfer and deliver all articles of personal and household use or ornament and all vehicles and accessories thereto, then owned by me.

As you can see, you can use the, vesting clause/transfer of property to the executor, to create unlimited specific trusts with details related to the property and the beneficiary. When all of your property is collected by your Executor it can be distributed in the following order; debts, taxes, funeral expenses, specific bequests, the residual estate.

7. Debts, Taxes and Testamentary Expenses Clause

This clause directs the executor to pay your debts, any funeral and testamentary expenses, income taxes, administration costs, or other expenses coming due. In most jurisdictions there is an obligation to pay debts of the estate first from capital, realized accounts and property, before any distribution to beneficiaries.

This clause can be used in conjunction with other clauses such as the Vesting Clause/Transfer of property to the Executor and the Residue Clause, as debts should be paid before specific trusts are dealt with. See example 2 below with basic Residue Clause and Example 5 with Vesting Clause and Residue Clause. The order of certain clauses in a Will can vary, best to keep in mind how they flow. (See section of **Residue Clause**.)

If your debts exceed your assets, there will be rules or law in your jurisdiction as to which debts have priority. Most commonly it is the funeral expenses first, then the administration expenses and finally, the general debts. An executor can be held liable if funds are paid out of the estate, and there are no remaining funds to pay for the funeral expenses.

If you have assets that are subject to tax, you must be careful. A named beneficiary can receive full market value of a cottage, cabin, registered account, business, et cetera, and the tax or debt liability can fall to the estate to pay. (i.e. A cottage valued at $200,000 passes to a named beneficiary, a registered account of $200,000 passes to a 2nd named beneficiary. The taxes payable on the cottage capital gain falls to the estate i.e. $50,000, and the income taxes on the registered account falls to the estate i.e. $100,000. If there is a residual beneficiary of the estate, they will receive only what is remaining after the $50,000 + $100,000 = $150,000, plus other obligations are paid.)

If any of these points affect you, I would recommend a conversation with a Certified Financial Planner to discuss:

- Debts of the estate,
- Debts on assets, such as a mortgage or chattel
- Income tax on registered plans and the effect to the estate
- Business interest(s) which may not be part of the estate and may have debts owing

[Example 7.1 (Debts, taxes and testamentary expenses clause)

I instruct my executor to pay my debts, funeral and testamentary expenses.

[Example 7.2 (Debts, taxes and testamentary expenses clause)

I give all my property to my [relationship - husband/wife/common law spouse/son/daughter/friend/lawyer, et cetera.],_____, after my debts, funeral and testamentary expenses are paid.

[Example 7.3 (Debts, taxes and testamentary expenses clause)

I direct my executor to pay from the capital of my estate, my enforceable debts, my funeral expenses, my testamentary expenses, my income taxes, and all my estate, legacy, succession or inheritance duties and/or taxes imposed pursuant to the laws of any jurisdiction in connection with any of my property, my accounts or my contracts upon my death.

[Example 7.4 (Debts, taxes and testamentary expenses clause)

I give, devise and bequeath all my property of every nature and kind and wherever situate, including any property over which I may have a general power of appointment, to my said Executor upon the following trusts, namely:

I direct my executor to pay from the capital of my estate, my enforceable debts, my funeral expenses, my testamentary expenses, my income taxes, and all my estate, legacy, succession or inheritance duties and/or taxes imposed pursuant to the laws of any jurisdiction in connection with any of my property, my accounts or my contracts upon my death.

I leave the residue of my estate to my [relationship - husband/wife/common law spouse/son/daughter/friend/lawyer, et cetera.],_____, if living on the 30th day following my death.

8. Residue Clause

The residue of the estate is everything remaining after all of the administration expenses, debts, taxes, bequests, specific assets, bequests and other dispositions have been paid out and there are no other known obligations or claims.

[Example 8.1 (Residue Clause)

I leave the residue of my estate to my [relationship - husband/wife/common law spouse/son/daughter/friend/lawyer, et cetera.],_____ if living on the 30th day following my death.

[Example 8.2 (Residue Clause)

I leave the residue of my estate to be divided equally between my children, _____ and _____.

[Example 8.3 (Residue Clause)

All the rest, residue and remainder of my estate of every kind whatsoever and wheresoever situate, I give to my [relationship - husband/wife/common law spouse/son/daughter/friend/lawyer, et cetera.],_____, absolutely if living on the 30th day following my death.

[
Example 8.4 (Residue Clause)

I give, devise and bequeath the residue of my estate, both real and personal, of every nature and kind and wheresoever situate, including any property over which I may have a general power of appointment, to my [relationship - husband/wife/common law spouse/son/daughter/friend/lawyer, et cetera.],_____, if he/she survives me for a period of [thirty (30) days], for his/her, own use absolutely.

9. Powers for Executor(s) and Trustee(s) to Act

The Will should also provide the executor and/or the trustees with wide powers to invest, manage and sell property, to borrow, to lend, to make income tax elections, to pay debts and expenses, to forgive loans, the power to retain agents and advisors for assistance - at his/her discretion. The executor or trustees may be subject to jurisdictional rules and not be able to take advantage of all options available if these powers are not included.

All trusts can give or expand the powers of the executor and trustees to act. It is important to give careful consideration to these powers to allow the executor and trustees to act flexibly in administering the trust assets. Some of these powers include the following:

- **General power of management and disposition.** The executor(s) or trustee(s) may carry out any transaction relating to the management or disposition of the assets of the trust as if they were the absolute owner of the assets. This power may include some of the following powers given its general nature, however, more detail in direction is often recommended.
- **Investments.** Some jurisdictional rules can be restrictive to trusts on the type of investments that are allowed. Consider giving the trustee(s) discretionary or broader powers to invest in 'prudent' assets that are considered practical for the administration of the trust over time and the discretion to delegate investment decisions to professional investment advisors.
- **Payments from trusts.** The executor can decide on when and how to pay debts and expenses, when to pay out all or partial income to beneficiaries, and also to encroach on capital as required or at their discretion.
- **To sell, transfer and/or retain business assets.** Business shares and real estate assets require wide-ranging rules to be managed properly. The executor can be given discretionary power so they can carry on the business, incorporate other assets, manage assets as a shareholder, exercise voting rights, give proxies, etc.
- **To sell, transfer and/or retain real estate assets.** Real estate assets can also require wide-ranging rules to be managed properly. The executor can be given discretionary power so they can borrow against, subdivide, clear land, allow family to remain in a house, time to calculate capital gains or other taxes on personal, recreation or rental properties, et cetera.

- **Borrow or lend money.** Your executor can arrange loans to beneficiaries at preferred rates, borrow until assets are sold, renew or continue debt obligations, manage mortgages on trust property, et cetera.

- **Deal with legal matters.** Commence, defend, arbitrate, and settle legal claims or actions concerning the estate or the assets and property in the estate;

- **Make income tax elections.** With good estate planning estates and trusts are often set up for tax saving purposes. Rules vary in jurisdictions and executors should be able to make income tax elections and decisions.

- **Executor entitlement to compensation.** Executors should be compensated for their time and effort, otherwise they may decline to act. The executors should be entitled to pay themselves according to local guidelines or regulations or specific to a testators wishes. Consider a 'gift', a fee or a percentage indicated in the Will.

- **Retain and/or employ professionals, experts, or advisors.** Experts and/or professionals may be required for the executor to get an understanding of assets, and complicated or specific tasks. They may need assistance with the ongoing investment of estate or trust assets, dealing with complicated tax matters, dealing with legal matters, insurance coverages and renewals, real estate maintenance or sales, and/or administration of estate paperwork.

- **Open and close various types of accounts.** Accounts may be needed for a variety of purposes such as an estate and/or trust account to collect and pay out funds. Estate brokerage and investment accounts to hold investments until sold, cashed or paid out. The executor may need this power to execute documents such as resolutions or certificates required for such accounts.

- **The power to hold assets for minors.** If you name a minor as a beneficiary under your Will, the law often says that the gift must be sold, money gifted, and funds must be paid into court or to a public trustee to be held until the child reaches the age of majority. To avoid this without creating a formal testamentary trust you can give your executor(s) absolute discretion and power to manage and distribute income and/or capital from the gift. (See **'Clauses for Minors'**.)

- **Executors release from liability.** This is to protect the executors from being sued, or from claims by beneficiaries in carrying out the powers above in their discretion, except from fraud or gross negligence. For example, a beneficiary can try to sue if an investment loss occurs. When assets are complex - market values can regularly change, liquidation may take time, and there are often limited things an executor can do.

- **Record keeping.** Executors should keep good records of all transactions related to the estate.

Example 9.1 (Powers and fiduciary obligations of executor(s) clause)

My Executor(s) is given all of the powers deemed necessary to administer the estate, including all powers granted under this jurisdiction's law, subject to the executor's fiduciary duties to the beneficiaries and any restrictions or limits set forth under this jurisdiction's law. The powers of the executor include, but are not limited to:

    i.   *Collect, manage, and _invest_ estate assets, the accumulation and distribution of income and principal, in any form of property in which a prudent investor might invest;*

ii.   _Borrow_ or lend money from the estate for estate purposes;

iii. Engage _agents_ and professionals in their discretion to assist in the administration of the estate;

iv.   Establish and administer any, bank, brokerage, other financial, and nonfinancial _accounts_ for and on behalf of the estate;

v.   Manage, operate, exercise obligations or sell any _business_ that is an estate asset;

vi.   Manage, sell, mortgage or lease any _real_ or leasehold property that forms part of my estate;

vii. Deal with _legal_ claims or actions concerning the estate or the assets and property in the estate;

viii. Prepare _tax_ returns, make income tax elections and take any necessary or desirable actions with governmental agencies;

ix.   My executor shall be fully exempt from any _liability_ or loss to my estate due to any decision made under these powers in good faith. These powers do not include exoneration for fraud or gross negligence.

x.   I hereby declare that each of my executors shall receive $_____ payable from the capital of the residue of my estate, as compensation for their acting as executors under this my _Will_.

More examples of powers to act can be found under Trusts, **Powers for Trustee/Trustee(s) to Act.**

10. Guardian(s), Conservators and/or Custodians

A guardian is someone who is usually legally responsible for the care of another. It can be a minor child, a person with a disability, an incapacitated individual, also known as a ward, etc. The terms conservator and custodian can be interchanged with guardian in many jurisdictions, we will use the term guardian to refer to all.

A guardian, conservator or protector should be named in a Will for minor children, and/or an incapacitated or disabled dependent, as your choice in a Will can carry a lot of weight in any court proceedings. Custody usually has to be confirmed by a court order, and those named can become 'Legal' when appointed or approved by a court.

Guardianship can be a complicated issue. Our discussion is limited to the basics of guardianship when it comes to minor children. If you have complex guardianship issues to resolve, for minors or for an incapacitated or disabled dependent, you may wish to find sources of more detailed information, or seek the help of a professional.

It should be noted that only a parent with sole custody can name a guardian in most jurisdictions, joint and shared custody situations should be addressed appropriately.

The legal guardian could also be given guardianship of property for minor children and the legally disabled. If the parents die before minors reach the age of majority, they may be designated to manage this property appropriately for the benefit of the children. The same goes for a disabled beneficiary. This can be accomplished with a basic clause, such as the examples below, in add-ons. If there is a need for more detailed instructions, such as when there are significant assets, a trust for minors should be considered. (See the following section **'Testamentary Trusts for Minors'** under Trusts.)

For children, guardians et al have a legal responsibility to the 'person' (child) for the daily care, upbringing and decision making related to health care, education, religion, activities, et cetera. Responsibility for 'property' may fall under other regulations, and it is usually recommended that provisions and instructions be provided in a Will for a trust to deal with property. Without a Will a child may be entitled to receive the estate upon attaining the age of majority, which most experts consider to still be too young to receive considerable assets.

Parents do not usually have to be appointed as legal guardians, and usually a surviving parent becomes guardian if they have been cohabiting or they share custody. It can be suggested that if you are separated or share custody that you make the other parent the guardian in writing in case something happens and to avoid another relative from applying for guardianship for some reason. If both parents die, a legal guardian will have to be appointed. A parent with sole custody who does not want the other parent as guardian should seek legal advice, as most parents would be appointed unless the court rules he or she is unsuitable.

In choosing an appropriate guardian you should consider those who:
- Would have a similar parenting style,
- Share the same values and religious beliefs,
- Are capable of taking on the care of a child, financially, physically and emotionally,
- Are very familiar to your child, or is a close family member,
- Are considered in a strong relationship unlikely to separate or divorce, if naming a couple.

Many jurisdictional courts make or confirm the final decision on who will be the legal guardian of minor children. Parent(s) should state their preference in the Will as it can be very persuasive in any proceedings.

Guardians for incapacitated or the mentally handicapped adults also have to follow jurisdictional procedures to be appointed legal guardian.

People can name more than one guardian if deemed necessary, and also name an alternate in case the others for some reason do not or cannot accept the responsibility.

You also have the option to provide specific instructions in your Will to your chosen guardian on religious beliefs, cultural preferences or other items that provide more relative guidance for your guardian in future decision making. You may also want include instructions on health care matters such as medical treatments for your children, however you may want to discuss these in advance with your physician or child's physician.

You should also include details on compensation for guardian(s), or detail how you feel about this.

A memorandum for guardianship can also be created detailing the wishes of the parent(s). It is not usually legally binding, but a court could consider the intentions of the parent(s) in making a decision.

[Example 10.1 (Naming Guardian(s))

I hereby appoint to serve as guardian without bond, over the persons and properties of my minor children, the following people in the following priority:

1) *My [relationship - husband/wife/common law spouse/son/daughter/friend/lawyer, et cetera.],*
   _____

2) *My [relationship - husband/wife/common law spouse/son/daughter/friend/lawyer, et cetera.],*
   _____

[Example 10.2 (Naming Guardian(s))

If my [relationship - husband/wife/common law spouse,], predeceases me, I appoint my [relationship – uncle/aunt/cousin/son/daughter/friend/lawyer, et cetera.],_____ as guardian of my minor children.

If for any reason _____ cannot act as guardian, I appoint my [relationship – uncle/aunt/cousin/son/daughter/friend/lawyer, et cetera.], _____ as guardian of my minor children.

Any person named as a guardian or custodian is not required to post any security or bond.

11. Clauses for Minors

Clauses for minors can be used in circumstances that do not require the use of a detailed trust. They can be used for when you choose to keep things simple, there are small gift amounts or when small amounts can be given to someone else to hold for the minor, and/or when the funds will be exhausted in a short time.

[Example 11.1 (Simple, without the need for a detailed testamentary trust.)

If any person should become entitled to any share in my estate before attaining the age of majority, the share of such person shall be held by my executor, and the income and capital or any part, as my executor in his absolute discretion considers advisable, shall be used for the benefit of such person until he or she attains the age of majority, and the remainder then paid to said beneficiary. If said beneficiary dies before the share is exhausted, it should be divided in equal shares per stirpes among his or her descendants who survive him or her.

[Example 11.2 (Simple to a guardian, without the need for a detailed testamentary trust.)

I authorize my Executor to make any payments for any beneficiary under the age of majority to such beneficiary's parent, guardian, or other legal representative whose receipt shall be sufficient discharge to my said Executor.

12. Bequests/Legacies/Devise(s)

A bequest is usually made when someone gives tangible personal property, a legacy is usually when someone gives money to a person or charity, and a divise is a clause giving real property; land or real estate through a Will. Bequest and legacy are often used interchangeably.

Devises can be complicated or troublesome for many estates if not direct to surviving spouse or an individual beneficiary. With real property; zoning/areas can be changed, real estate properties require maintenance, people move on, shared ownership can become troublesome on disagreements, etc. You would have to provide several provisions and more details to avoid these issues.

Consider if it is best to sell real estate, unless going to a surviving spouse or single person. If given to multiple parties as a shared asset it would be best to give options of a shared devise to be bought out by the first offer for value that is unmatched (i.e. Shotgun clause). Your intentions should be especially very clear when there is a mortgage or encumbrance on the property. (See ' Add-on' clauses.) Professional help should be sought if the executor is not given the power and discretion to sell any real property.

If you want to leave tangible personal property such as a family heirloom, china collection, in-kind donations to a charity or foundation; or any specific, personal, non-monetary item to a specific person or organization, you would include it as a bequest. It is important to leave sufficient detail about the bequest/legacy/devise so that the item or amount is easily identified or determined.

A bequest or legacy can be made conditional on an event or situation. i.e. 'provided William is neither incarcerated nor incapacitated', 'provided William does not predecease me'.

Bequests/legacies should be reviewed to ensure they are still applicable over time.
- Ademption can occur when a bequeathed asset is no longer in the estate. The gift to the beneficiary fails and there is no other entitlement unless specified.
- Abatement can occur when there are not enough funds to satisfy legacies or gifts, so a proportional reduction may have to be made.

With charitable bequests or legacies, it is very important to be very clear when making a gift as it is their duty to ensure it has received its intended donation. A charity my request a review of the administration of an estate if the details of the donation are not clear; especially if the charity is a residual beneficiary, meaning the proper administration of the estate can determine what their entitlement is.

Consider leaving a specific dollar amount to a charity so you can easily avoid these issues. For example, 'I would like to leave a legacy of exactly $10,000 to my favorite charity The Favorite Charity in city, province/state, country, registration #11111111.' Charitable bequests have tax benefits in most jurisdictions.

Bequests:

[Example 12.1

I bequeath my mother's wedding ring, to my [relationship - husband/wife/common law spouse/son/daughter/friend/lawyer, et cetera.], _____

[Example 12.2

I bequeath my guitar to my [relationship - husband/wife/common law spouse/son/daughter/friend/lawyer, et cetera.], _____

[Example 12.3

I bequeath my car to my [relationship - husband/wife/common law spouse/son/daughter/friend/lawyer, et cetera.], _____

Legacies:

[Example 12.4

I leave a legacy of 'Amount' to 'Name' of 'Address'.

[Example 12.5

I leave a legacy of exactly $10,000 to my friend 'Name' of 'Address'.

[Example 12.6

I leave a legacy of exactly $10,000 to my friend _____, of 'Permanent Residence and Jurisdiction', provided (he/she) survives me.

[Example 12.7

'I leave a legacy of exactly $10,000 to my favorite charity 'Charity Name' at 'Full Address', registration number '#'.

Devise(s):

[Example 12.8

To my [relationship - husband/ wife/ common law spouse/ son/ daughter/ friend/ lawyer, et cetera.],
_____, *I devise and give the real property located at 'Address of Residence in Jurisdiction',*
provided he/ she survives me, together with all furniture, appliances, dishes, silverware, art work; permanently maintained in
the property, and tools necessary for the maintenance and operation of the property.

Add-ons: (For mortgages, debts, or taxes.)

If you leave certain assets to beneficiaries, you should decide and indicate if a beneficiary is to pay the tax, or the estate is to pay the tax. See your Certified Financial Planner to review these items if they apply to you.

[Example 12.9

All beneficiaries receiving specific property shall be responsible for any encumbrances such as mortgages, debts, or taxes on the transfer of ownership.

[Example 12.10

If any of the real property devised in my Wills remains subject to a mortgage at the time of my death, then I direct that the devisee will be responsible for that mortgage, and the mortgage shall not be paid from the residue of my estate.

13. Trusts

In simplest terms in common law legal systems, a trust is a relationship whereby property; is given by one party, the settlor, to be held by another party, the trustee, for the benefit of another party, the beneficiary.

An owner, the settlor, who transfer property into a trust turns over the property's legal ownership and control to the trustee(s). This may be done for tax reasons or to control the property and its benefits if the settlor is absent, incapacitated, or deceased.

A trustee can be a person, a company or a government body. There can be a single trustee or multiple co-trustees. The trustee is obligated to act for the good of the beneficiaries. The trustee may be compensated and have expenses reimbursed, but otherwise must manage income and trust property for the beneficiaries benefit.

Common responsibilities of the trustee:
- Prudently manage and invest the trust property;
- Avoid conflicts of interest;
- Act with an even hand towards beneficiaries, treat all equally, unless stipulated in trust document;
- Avoid improper delegation of authority;
- Inform beneficiaries of their entitlements;
- Sell trust property as required;

- Pay the trust's debts and taxes.

Trusts are frequently created in Wills, defining how money and property will be handled for children or other beneficiaries. The Will may establish the terms of any trusts to be created upon death.

Many people consider trusts to be a vehicle for the wealthy and to manage complicated affairs. However, this is not really the case. An example of a trust in the simplest of uses in a Will is, 'I leave all my assets in trust for my children.' With this, the executor or can set up a trust for the children and the trust will be managed according to the jurisdictional rules. This can lead to many problems and complications, i.e Minor children may not have access to funds until the age of majority. What if there are claims by children born outside of wedlock, what would the testator have wanted? When can assets like a house/the home, land, cottage, or cabin be sold? et cetera. See the powers you can give your trustees below to add substance and direction to this trust or similar.

The reasons for settling a trust are numerous, however trust legislation and taxation are constantly changing in many jurisdictions and it is outside the scope of this workbook to provide anything but an introduction to trusts.

From this introduction you will get an idea on how trusts can work. We will explain some of the most popular uses for trusts in estate and tax planning, family planning, and providing for minors or disabled beneficiaries.

The trust is governed by the terms under which it was created. In most jurisdictions, this requires a contractual trust agreement, deed or a properly drafted Will.

For a trust to be valid in most jurisdictions it must show three certainties:
1. Certainty of Intention: it should be clear that the donor or settlor intends to create a trust;
2. Certainty of subject matter: it should be clear what property is to be part of the trust and each of the beneficiaries' interest can be defined;
3. Certainty of objects: it should be clear who the objects or beneficiaries are.

There are two main types of trusts, *Inter vivos* or living trust, and testamentary trust.

Inter vivos trust or living trust:

A settlor who is living at the time the trust is established creates an *inter vivos* trust or living trust.

Some common uses of living trusts:
- Provide income to children of a previous marriage or relationship
- Provide income to an ex-spouse based on a divorce or separation agreement

- Manage assets for someone who lacks financial expertise
- Manage assets and/or income for a disabled or incapacitated person
- To hold or manage a gift to minors, other dependent or a legally disabled person
- Tax planning opportunities (Constantly changing)
- To provide future gifts or donations to charities
- Avoid probate, estate fees and/or taxes
- To keep asset information confidential

A common inter vivos trust is a revocable trust. It can be used to avoid probate, allow the settlor to manage assets during his lifetime, to keep information private, etc.

In a revocable trust the grantor/settlor can have assets held or removed during his/her lifetime, make changes or cancel provisions of the trust, receive income from the trust, and then on death of the grantor the assets can be held for or transferred to the beneficiaries.

The trust then becomes an irrevocable trust. The trust provisions cannot be changed.

See your Certified Financial Planner to discuss your estate planning using inter vivos trusts, their cost and maintenance, and other pros and cons for your specific situation.

Testamentary Trusts:

Testamentary Trusts are usually created in Wills; a testamentary trust is created when control over certain property is transferred to the trustee(s) on the death of the settlor to hold for a beneficiary.

Testamentary trusts allow for three main objectives:
1) Income splitting,
2) Control beyond the grave,
3) Creditor protection of the beneficiaries.

Some common uses of testamentary trusts:
- Provide for a minor beneficiary;
- Provide income or living interest to a surviving spouse;
- Manage assets for beneficiaries who lack financial expertise;
- Manage assets and/or income for a disabled or incapacitated person;
- Manage assets for a spendthrift or incarcerated person;
- Tax planning opportunities (Constantly changing);
- To provide future gifts or donations to charities;
- To protect beneficiaries against creditor claims.

Testamentary trusts can also be created separate from a Will in a life insurance policy by naming the beneficiary of the policy 'a trust for a person or persons'. The terms of such a trust can be detailed in a Will or in a trust agreement and a copy provided to the insurance issuer.

If you name a minor as a beneficiary under a life insurance policy, the law often says that the gift must be sold, money gifted, and funds must be paid into court or to a public trustee to be held until the child reaches the age of majority. To avoid this you can create a testamentary trust, separate from other dispositions in the Will, and it specifies the insurance policy. Care should be taken with life insurance trusts, as you do not wish proceeds of life insurance to flow through the estate and be subjected to estate taxes or probate fees. See your CFP.

Testamentary Trusts for Minors

A testamentary trust can be used to hold property for the benefit of minor children until they reach the age of majority or later, for other dependents or legally disabled beneficiaries. It is outside the scope of this book to address all the issues related to minor children, other dependents or legally disabled beneficiaries. We will address minor beneficiaries, as it the most common need.

The trust should give the trustees discretion to invest and provide income or capital to the guardians of the children to pay for ongoing expenses for maintenance, for educational or recreational programs, for medical care and for opportunities for the children.

Testamentary trusts should be used to postpone the ultimate receipt of property from an estate until children or grandchildren have reached a more mature age than simply the age of majority. This ensures that the children on reaching the age of majority are not given a large sum or assets that they may not know how to manage properly.

Trustees can be given the power to pay for any post-secondary education, lump sum for a wedding, a car, a down payment, et cetera. The trustees can be given the power and task of winding down the trust when the child is a mature adult and/or capable of managing the remaining funds. You can choose an age or various ages for lump sum distributions, you can choose a partial distribution each year of income and/or capital, up until a specific age for final division or distribution of all assets, or you can leave it to the discretion of the trustees to determine a time.

Similar trusts can be created for the other dependents and/or the legally disabled, with specific instructions for each situation. Planning for disabled beneficiaries can be very complex; it is recommended you review your situation with a Certified Financial Planner (CFP).

(a) Appointing a Trustee or Trustees

If your executor(s) are to act as your trustees for specific trusts, the previous appointment should be sufficient. See **'Appoint an Executor/Estate Representative'**.

If you wish to appoint different trustees or a second trustee with the executor, you can review these clauses.

[Example 13.1 (Single trustee)

I appoint _____ to serve as Trustee of any trust created under this my Will, and if my Trustee is unwilling or unable to serve, I appoint _____ to serve as the Successor Trustee of any trust created under this my Will.

[Example 13.2 (Two trustees)

I appoint _____ and _____, as Co-Trustees of any trust created under this my Will, and if either of them is unwilling or unable to serve, the remaining Co-Trustee to continue to serve as sole successor Trustee hereunder. I request my Co-Trustees make every reasonable effort to make their decisions unanimously, however, in the event they are unable to do so, _____ shall have the ultimate decision making authority.

Add-on: (Excluding someone as a trustee)

[Example 13.3

I do not want _____ to serve as my Trustee under any circumstances.

(b) Testamentary Trusts for Minors

[Example 13.4 (Trust for minor with executor and another trustee.)

I name my said executor and _____ as Trustees, to hold in trust the share of any minor, and to keep such share invested, pay the income or capital or as much of either or both as my trustees considers available for the maintenance, education, advancement or benefit of such minor, and to pay or transfer the capital of such share or the amount remaining of that share to such minor beneficiary when he or she reaches the age of majority.

[Example 13.5 (Trust for minor with executors previously appointed (executors are trustees).)

Without restricting the absolute discretion of my Trustees with respect to the payment of income and capital for the benefit of minor beneficiaries, I wish to emphasize to my Trustees that I consider it very important that liberal payments be made to the guardians of minor beneficiaries from the income or capital or as much of either or both as my trustees considers available for the maintenance, education, advancement or benefit of such minor.

To pay or transfer the capital of such share or the amount remaining of that share to such minor beneficiary when he or she reaches the age of majority.

[Example 13.6 (Trust for minors with executor and another trustee.)

I name my said executor and _____ as Trustees, of all Testamentary Trusts required in my Will.

Any assets bequeathed, transferred, or gifted to a minor beneficiary named in my Will are to be held in a separate trust by the Trustees.

Without restricting the absolute discretion of my Trustees with respect to the payment of income and capital for the benefit of such minor beneficiary, I wish to emphasize to my Trustees that I consider it very important that liberal payments be made to the guardians of minor beneficiaries from the income or capital or as much of either or both as my trustees considers available for the maintenance, education, advancement or benefit of such minor.

Any property left by me to any minor beneficiary in my Will will be given to my trustees to be managed until that minor reaches the age of majority, whereby they will receive 25% of remaining funds, age 25 they will receive 50% of remaining funds, age 30 they shall receive all of the remaining funds and the trust shall be dissolved or wound down.

[Example 13.7 (Trust for minors with executor(s).)

All property left in this my Will, to my [relationship - son/daughter/niece/nephew/grandchild, etc.], _____, shall be held in trust for him/her.

My Trustee shall set aside his/her share as a separate trust and shall keep such share invested and, may from time to time until he/she becomes absolutely entitled to all the capital, pay to or apply the benefit to the beneficiary, any of the income and the capital or part of, as my Trustee in his absolute discretion deem advisable from time to time remaining in trust.

Upon my [relationship - son/daughter/niece/nephew/grandchild, etc.], _____ attaining the age of 25 years, such share or the amount then remaining shall be paid or transferred to him/her.

If my [relationship - son/daughter/niece/nephew/grandchild, etc.], , _____ should die before receiving all the capital of him/her share, such share or the amount then remaining shall be divided among the descendants of him/her who shall be living at the death of the survivor of him/her in equal shares per stirpes. If my [relationship - son/daughter/niece/nephew/grandchild, etc.], , _____ should leave no descendants surviving, such share shall be added to the residue of my estate.

[Example 13.8 (Insurance Trust for minors with one trustee.)

I,_____, declare that the proceeds of my insurance policy number, _____ issued by Insurance Company, _____, shall be paid to my insurance trustee, _____, as a separate Insurance Trust Fund for my [relationship - son/daughter/niece/nephew/grandchild, etc.], _____, and [relationship - son/daughter/niece/nephew/grandchild, etc.], _____,

The Insurance Trust Fund shall be divided by the Insurance Trustee into as many equal shares as may be required in order that there is one equal share for each of my children, who survives me and I direct my Insurance Trustees to hold the Insurance Proceeds for the benefit of those children on the following trusts:

a. My Insurance Trustee shall set aside his/her share as a separate trust and shall keep such share invested and, may from time to time until he/she becomes absolutely entitled to all the capital, pay to or apply the benefit to the beneficiary, any of the income and the capital or part of as my Trustee in his absolute discretion deem advisable from time to time. Upon my [relationship - son/daughter/niece/nephew/grandchild, etc.], _____ attaining the age of 25 years, such share or the amount then remaining shall be paid or transferred to him/her;

b. If any of my children should die before receiving the entire benefit of the Insurance Proceeds, the Insurance Proceeds or the amount remaining shall be paid or transferred to his or her children alive at the date of his or her death in equal shares, or if there is no such children of him or her then alive, then the Insurance Proceeds or the amount remaining shall be divided in equal shares amongst my children then living and invested in accordance with paragraph (a) above.

The Insurance Trustees shall have the same powers and obligations as my executor(s) and other trustee(s) have for the administration of my estate pursuant to the terms of this my Will.

The wording of these clauses can be edited, added, taken away to fit any particular situation desired, such as number and names of beneficiaries, while maintaining the substance of the directions needed to carry out your wishes.

Trust Termination - The Testamentary Trust can end after any of the following:

- The minor beneficiary reaches the age set for final distribution;
- The minor beneficiary dies;
- The assets of the trust are exhausted through distributions;
- Or you can set a perpetuity date or time period for the trust to be wound down, i.e. 21 years, 30 years, etc.

Testamentary trusts can also be used to hold property such as a home or cottage for the benefit of a beneficiary or a number of beneficiaries for a period of time, such as a home or cottage. It is important to leave funds available for maintenance, repairs, property taxes and other expenses related to this type of property or more detailed instructions on how these expenses are to be paid.

Example 13.9 (Life interest trust clause for a common law spouse.)

I give to my [relationship - husband/wife/common law spouse/son/daughter/friend/lawyer, et cetera.], _____ , my dwelling house and land, subject to the right of my common-law spouse, _____ to live in, occupy and possess the same as her place of dwelling until he/she enters into another relationship of a spousal nature, vacates the property, or otherwise decides to relinquish his/her rights as herein provided.

It is advisable to seek help in dealing with a life interest in a property, such as a life interest in a home to a spouse, a cottage to children, a home to one child, etc. If clear directions are not set out a person or persons with the life interest can decide to let the property fall into disrepair or neglect, which is obviously not the original intention.

(c) Powers for Trustee/Trustee(s) to Act

As covered under **Powers for Executor(s) or Trustee(s) to Act;** all trusts can give or expand the powers of the executor and trustees to act. These powers were discussed under the above as executors are trustees and these powers are much the same. We will not duplicate the information here, but add a few more examples in different format, you can go back and review that section for more information and clarity.

Some of these powers as mentioned include the following:

- Investments.
- Payments from trusts.
- To sell, transfer and/or retain assets.
- Borrow or lend money.
- Make income tax elections.

- Entitlement to compensation.
- Retain and/or employ professionals.
- Open and close various types of accounts.
- Release from liability.
- Hold assets for minors.

When you create specific trusts and/or name additional trustees you should include the powers again for those trustees, under the clause appointing the trustee, or the clause creating the trust. Additional examples of giving powers to trustees follow. It is highly recommended when creating a trust to seek professional assistance.

[Example 13.10 (Powers for Trustee(s) and/or Executor(s))

In order to carry out the trusts of my Will, I give my Executor and/or trustee(s) the following powers in addition to <u>jurisdictional powers</u> to be used in the exercise of an absolute discretion at any time:

To pay my legally enforceable <u>debts</u>, funeral expenses and all expenses in connection with the administration of my estate and trusts created by my Will as soon as convenient after my death.

To take all <u>legal</u> actions to maintain, settle, abandon, sue or defend, against my estate; and as free as possible from any court supervision, under the law of this jurisdiction.

To retain, exchange, insure, repair, improve, sell or dispose of any and all tangible <u>personal property</u> belonging to my estate as my Executor deems advisable.

To invest, manage, lease, rent, exchange, mortgage, sell, dispose of or give options without being limited to term and to insure, repair, improve, or add to or otherwise deal with any and all <u>real property</u> belonging to my estate as my Executor deems advisable. If any of the real property devised in my Will remains subject to a mortgage at the time of my death, then I direct that the devisee will be responsible for that mortgage, and the mortgage shall not be paid from the residue of my estate.

To open or close <u>accounts</u> such as an estate, brokerage, investment and/or trust accounts; to purchase, maintain, convert and liquidate any savings , investments or securities, to vote stock, or exercise any option concerning any accounts, investments or securities.

To maintain, manage, dissolve, change or sell any <u>business</u> which is part of my estate by my executor.

To retain or employ investment counsel, lawyer, accountant, other <u>agents</u> or advisors for the ongoing investment of estate or trust assets, dealing with complicated tax matters, dealing with legal matters, insurance coverages and renewals, real estate maintenance and sales, or the general administration of the estate or trust.

My Trustees shall be fully exempt from any <u>liability</u> or loss to my estate due to any decision made under these powers in good faith. These powers do not include exoneration for fraud or gross negligence.

My trustees are authorized to accept <u>compensation</u> payments according to local guidelines or regulations.

Example 13.11 (Powers for Trustee(s) and/or Executor(s))

In addition to the powers given to my trustees by the <u>laws of this jurisdiction</u> without restrictions, I give that my Trustees shall have the power, discretion and authority to deal with the assets held by this trust and without the interference of any person entitled under my Will, as follows:

In making investments for my estate, my trustees may <u>invest</u> the assets of my estate in 'prudent' assets that are considered practical for the administration of the trust over time. My trustees have to power to hire professional investment counsel or advisors if them deem necessary.

In relation to my <u>real estate assets</u>, to sell, mortgage, lease, pay expenses for maintenance and repairs, as they consider appropriate until such time as the real estate assets can be sold in the best interest of my estate.

In relation to with my <u>business assets</u>, to sell, retain, reorganize or carry on the business, as they consider appropriate until such time as the assets can be sold or transferred, in the best interest of my estate.

In relation to any of my estate assets, to transfer them <u>in specie</u> or in kind, as they consider appropriate until such time as the assets can be sold or transferred, in the best interest of my estate.

In relation to my estate, to retain <u>professional agents</u> to assist in trust administration matters, delegate certain tasks to such agents as they consider appropriate, and pay these agents from the capital and income of the estate.

In relation to my estate, to <u>borrow</u> on behalf of my estate such amounts as my trustees consider appropriate, including and not limited to, loans to beneficiaries at preferred rates, borrow until assets are sold, renew or continue debt obligations, management of and any mortgages on trust property.

In relation to my estate, to deal with <u>legal</u> claims or actions related to my estate, and may make any agreement with any person or entity which shall be binding upon all persons with an interest in my estate.

In relation to my estate, to make any election, or designation, under the jurisdiction's <u>tax</u> rules and regulations, in the best interest of my estate.

My trustees are authorized in their discretion to accept <u>compensation</u> payments according to local guidelines or regulations.

My Trustees shall be fully exempt from any <u>liability</u> or loss to my estate due to any decision made under these powers in good faith. These powers do not include exoneration for fraud or gross negligence.

Proper Maintenance and Support to Spouse and Dependents

The Will should provide direction with respect to providing adequate support to spouses, children, or other dependents such as children outside of marriage, adopted, or stepchildren, and also dependent adults.

A surviving spouse often is entitled to a statutory share of your estate regardless of your Will. In some jurisdictions a surviving spouse is entitled by law to the family home as a homestead right. (They can volunteer to give these up in most prenuptial, marital, cohabitation or separation agreements.) This may not hold true for common law spouses and partners who are not legally married in many jurisdictions.

Regardless of what is written in the Will, most jurisdictions have laws that dictate a spousal share, homestead rights and methods for dependents to apply for support payments, so review your jurisdictions regulations. With prenuptial, marital, cohabitation or separation agreements, specific clauses may fail if they conflict with public policy.

A Spousal Trust , can be created in a Will to provide maintenance, support or life interest for surviving spouse or to reduce taxes. See the section **'Trusts',** for ideas on spousal and dependent support options using trusts.

Spousal and dependent support issues can be complex, and require a full analysis of the testator's current situation, including assets available, income needed, plans to hold assets, etc. It is best to review this issue with your Certified Financial Planner.

As you can see, there are many options in using trusts; however our discussion is limited to basic testamentary trusts that can be used in many situations and satisfy most basic needs. If 50% of the population do not have a Will or estate plan, they can use much of the previously discussed material and examples to create basic trusts and get their Wills completed.

14. Common Disaster, Gift Over, Failure, and/or Survival Clauses.

Common disaster, gift over, failure, and/or survival clauses are used in case of situations where spouses, partners and/or beneficiaries may die at the same time, within a short period of time of your death, or pre-decease you.

If spouses or partners without children are named as each other's beneficiaries; there can be complications if there isn't such a clause. (For example, let's say in a car accident, two spouses are seriously injured and then die within a few days of each other. The spouse who died second could inherit all from the spouse who died first, then his or her beneficiaries will inherit all. So if there are no children, only siblings of each as next of kin, the siblings of the person who died second could get all, and the siblings of the person who died first could get nothing.)

You can add-on a survival clause which includes a number of days where a spouse, partner or beneficiary has to survive you by, i.e. 30 days.

You can use a 'gift over' clause is to provide for the gift of property to pass to a second or subsequent recipient if a certain event occurs, such as the death of the first and/or second beneficiaries.

You can include a common disaster clause where each of the person's alternate beneficiaries would inherit.

We do not know what the future holds, and because of this we must plan for all that we can think of, and choose what suits you. A failure clause can deal with situations where a gift of assets for primary and contingent beneficiaries does not vest, or the residue clause fails due to a beneficiary(s) predeceasing the testator.

[Example 14.1 (Common disaster with survival)

*I give the whole of my estate to my [relationship - husband/wife/common law spouse/son/daughter/friend/, et cetera.],
_____ provided 'he/she' survives me by a period of thirty (30) days.*

*If my [relationship - husband/wife/common law spouse/son/daughter/friend/sibling, et cetera.],
_____ fails to survive me by thirty (30) days, I give the whole of my estate in equal shares to my [relationship – children/sibling, et cetera.], _____,
_____.*

If all previously named fail to survive me, I give the whole of my estate to my [relationship - husband/wife/common law spouse/son/daughter/friend/sibling, et cetera.],_____.

[Example 14.2 (Failure)

If any part of my estate should fail to vest, my trustee shall give this share to be divided in equal shares per stirpes amongst his/her/their descendants who survive him/her/them provided they are living at the final distribution date. If this fails it should be given to my next of kin. (See Table of Cansanguinity.)

[Example 14.3 (Gift Over)

If said beneficiary dies before the share is exhausted, it should be divided in equal shares per stirpes among his or her descendants who survive him or her.

Per stirpes is a term that refers to beneficiaries' roots. If a beneficiary dies, then the testator would like the beneficiaries' share to go to his/her children.

15. Divorce and Community/Family Property

In some jurisdictions you may want to state that any part of your estate (and its growth in value) that your children inherit will be separate from their family and/or community property depending on your jurisdictions rules. An inheriting adult child could have a divorce immediately following your death and end up losing one half of the inheritance to the ex-spouse.

Many jurisdictions now specify that inheritances do not form part of community or family property for the purposes of divorce, provided the assets are kept separate and apart. It is best to seek further advice if it applies to your situation.

[Example 15.1 (Divorce and community/family property clause)

I declare that all property acquired by any beneficiary under my Will, shall be excluded from such beneficiary's community property, net family property, partnership, and shall not be subject to claims of ownership or division by such beneficiary's spouse or partner pursuant to legislation of any jurisdiction, it being my intention that all property together with the income from this property shall remain the separate property of a beneficiary named, free from all matrimonial rights or controls by his or her spouse.

Children Born Outside of Wedlock

Traditionally under common law children born outside of wedlock, or known as an illegitimate child, had no legal right to inherit. Children may be treated differently depending on jurisdiction. Recently many jurisdictions have abolished illegitimacy and treat these children as equal beneficiaries to other children. It is important that your Will details your wishes relating to support and inheritance, if there is the possibility of a claim, or if you wish to expressly provide for such children. Professional help is advised.

16. Exclusion of a Person(s) from your Will

If you choose to exclude someone who would be considered a beneficiary or next-of-kin from your Will it is important to explain why in detail. It can reduce the possibility of arguments or any challenges to the Will later. Discuss with a lawyer.

[Example 16.1 (Exclusion of a person from your Will)

I do not wish for my [relationship – ex-husband/ex-wife/ex-common law spouse, estranged child, ex-friend, et cetera.],
_____, *to receive anything from my estate under any circumstances. My reasons being,*
_____.

17. Testimonial and Attestation Clauses/ Signature, and Witnesses to the Will

To ensure a properly executed Will, in most jurisdictions the testator declares to two witnesses that they are about to see him/her sign their Last Will and Testament, he/she the testator then signs the document, Testamonium. The witnesses then sign a short declaration in the Will that they were present and witnessed the testator's signature in each other's presence, Attestation. It can also include the number of pages in the Will and the date of signing.

A good practice is for the testator to begin by initialing each page of the Will in succession, each witness initial each page after the testator, then complete with the testator's signature and witness signatures in the appropriate areas. This can protect against insertions of pages in the Will later.

Most Wills except holograph Wills should be witnessed by two people in most jurisdictions. The witnesses should be '*disinterested*'; not a spouse of the testator or a beneficiary under the Will. A spouse or beneficiary could be disallowed from receiving under the Will, or they could invalidate their status as a witness. It is advised that you find witnesses who will not receive anything under the Will under any circumstances, or you risk voiding certain provisions in the Will, opening it to challenge, or possibly invalidating the entire will.

Once the Will is signed and witnessed properly, it becomes a legal Last Will and Testament. There is no requirement to have the document notarized, stamped, or signed by a lawyer. Nor does the document need to be registered.

It is also an important consideration at the time of witnessing to get an affidavit sworn and signed by at least one witness identifying the Will and attesting that they witnessed your signature on the Will. These are known in various jurisdictions as an affidavit of execution, affidavit – proof of Will. You may get an affidavit from both witnesses if it is convenient.

A self-proving affidavit, used in many states, is signed by the two witnesses and the testator at the same time the Will is executed. It is a statement that the testator is of age, is of sound mind and acted without undue influence, signed the Will, in the presence of the witnesses, who were also in the presence of each other.

You should know how many witnesses are required and which affidavit is appropriate for your jurisdiction. These have to be sworn in front of a lawyer, notary, commissioner of oaths, or justice of the peace.

These affidavits will save time and effort when the executor has to have the Will validated or probated and will need one of these types of affidavits. Significant delays in probate can occur if witnesses cannot be found or are deceased and there is no affidavit. (Sample affidavits are provided at the back of the book.)

[Example 17.1 (Testimonial and Attestation Clauses/ Signature, and Witnesses to the Will)

Signed by the testator in our joint presence and attested by us in the presence of him/her and of each other,

Testator, 'Full Name' Signature _____

1st Witness Signature _____

2nd Witness Signature _____

[Example 17.2 (Testimonial and Attestation Clauses/ Signature, and Witnesses to the Will)

I hereby sign my name to this my Last Will and Testament, written on these ____ pages of paper, this 'Date of Month' day of 'Month', 'Year'.

Signed, Published and Declared,
By the said Testator/Testatrix, _____,
                               (Print Full Name)

              _____

                   (Testator Signature)

In the presence of both of us at the same time, who at 'his/her' request, and in the presence of each other, have subscribed our names as witnesses.

_____, _____

Print Witness Name (1)   *Address 1*

_____,

Witness Signature

_____, _____

Print Witness Name (2)   *Address 1*

_____,

Witness Signature

[Example 17.3 (Testimonial and Attestation Clauses/ Signature, and Witnesses to the Will)

I hereby sign my name to this my Last Will and Testament, written on these ____ pages of paper, this 'Date of Month' day of 'Month', 'Year'.

Signed, Published and Declared,
By the said Testator, _____,
                  (Print Full Name)

              _____

(Testator Signature)

The foregoing instrument was signed, and declared by _____, the above-named Testator to be such Testator's Last Will and Testament in our presence, all being present at the same time, and we, at such Testator's request and in such Testator's presence and in the presence of each other, have subscribed our names as witnesses on the date above written.

_____, _____

Print Witness Name (1)   *Address 1*

_____,

Witness Signature

_____, _____

Print Witness Name (2)   *Address 1*

_____,

Witness Signature

18. Revising your Will with a Codicil

A Will should be revised after any of these occurrences,

- Marriage, divorce, separation or cohabitation. Most jurisdictions consider income and property acquired during the marriage as family property, which is usually equally divisible amongst spouses. Some jurisdictions include common-law and same-sex partners; it is advisable to check your jurisdiction's legislation.
- Change in status of a beneficiary or executor. If someone predeceases you, an executor moves out of jurisdiction, a revision may be in order.
- A child reaching age of majority. Children reaching age of majority have full access to any inheritance, if you do not wish this, you may consider a trust to spread the inheritance out over time, and include conditions.
- A change in jurisdiction, province/state/country. Most jurisdictions have different legislation.
- Assets acquired in another jurisdiction, or you can create another Will in that jurisdiction for those specific assets only.
- Disposition of specific or significant assets named in the Will. You do not want your executor searching for assets that do not exist, and/or beneficiaries questioning where assets named in a Will are.

A Will cannot be altered by crossing out or writing in new clauses, as they would need to be executed as the original Will.

Most changes to a Will can be done using a codicil, which is an amendment to the Will. It can contain information on any addition, explanation or modification of anything in the Will, can revoke a clause in your Will and then substitute a new clause, and is a totally separate document. I.e. Change of executor(s), beneficiary(s), bequests, legacies, guardian(s), or the transfer of an item.

The codicil will need to be signed and witnessed as with the original Will, however the witnesses need not be the same, and it is a good practice to get an affidavit by witnesses to the signature as with the original Will.

The contents of an Exordium clause of a codicil, similar to the original Will are likely to:

- Identify the testator/testatrix and should include any variation of the person's name, or aliases used to hold property.
- State a legal domicile - your permanent residence or intended residence in your jurisdiction, especially if you are living temporarily outside your jurisdiction.
- Include the testator's occupation.
- It should refer to the Last Will and Testament to which the Codicil relates and include the date the original Will was created, signed and witnessed.
- It can include a declaration of being of sound mind and body.
- It can include a declaration of not acting under duress or undue influence.
- It can also include revocation any clause in prior wills.

[Example 18.1 (Codicil)

I, being of sound mind and body do hereby declare that this document is a Codicil to the Last Will and Testament of 'First Name Middle Name Surname', of 'Permanent Residence and Jurisdiction', made this 'Date of Month' day of 'Month', 'Year'. 'Occupation'.

I confirm all clauses of my Will dated 'Date of Month' day of 'Month', 'Year', except that I add to it clause '1A' which is that set out below,

1A. 'Details of change'

Signed by the testator in our joint presence and attested by us in the presence of her and of each other;

Signed, Published and Declared,
By the said Testator, '_____,
(Full Name)

_____
(Testator Signature)

_____ ,,,, _____, _____
Witness Name (1)   *Address 1*

_____,

Witness Signature

_____ , _____

Witness Name (2)   *Address 1*

_____ ,

Witness Signature

c) Memorandums

A memorandum is an expression of wishes which can be added to your estate documents. Most estate trustees or executors will accept it as additional direction from the Will, but they are not usually legally binding. It is important to discuss with a lawyer in your jurisdiction how to make them legally binding.

Besides the personal property memorandum mentioned under bequests, where you list the names of beneficiaries for tangible personal property there are other types of memorandums:

- If creating a testamentary trust, you can create a memorandum of intent or wishes, to give greater direction to your trustees in making decisions; however, you should note in it that it is not to override the terms and powers of the trust.

- A memorandum for digital assets, this can contain all of your user names/identifications/IDs and passwords for accessing an account.

- You should also consider a memorandum for funeral instructions so that it is available immediately on death to those who need to make the arrangements, instead of waiting for the Will to be read.

- You can also use a memorandum for organ donation to express your wishes if you have not made other arrangements.

Make them accessible to family members immediately when needed, before the Will is read. If you plan to use memorandums, it is best to make them, date and sign before you execute your Will. Include a clause in your Will that refers to it. If you wish to ensure their legality, you should discuss with an estate lawyer.

[Example 19.1 (Memorandum)

I may leave a Tangible Personal Property Memorandum apart from this my Will, gifting of some or all of my tangible personal property. If I do so and the memorandum can be adjoined by this reference in this my Will, or otherwise be legally binding, I direct that it be adjoined or followed and prevail over the disposition in this my Will. This provision shall apply whether the writing is executed before or after this my Will.

d) Funeral Arrangements

Making funeral arrangements in advance, or at least discussing your wishes with family members, will relieve them of having to make these decisions after your death.

One good reason to do it in advance is the cost, last minute services are usually marked up, and it's not a good time to be shopping around, making emotional decisions. Pre-made arrangements which can be paid for later are often a good idea. Most funeral homes provide seminars so you can enlighten yourself on the choices beforehand, and shopping around early always helps. Funds can be placed in a trust fund to pay the costs later. The contract may be cancelled later and other arrangements made if desired. If you do prepay, get a copy of the contract, signed by both parties and detailing the items requested and the costs and terms associated.

A life insurance policy can also be purchased so that funds are available to cover funeral costs. This is an ideal option for young people, single people, those with limited funds available, or anyone else who can arrange reasonable premiums. Insurance can be available through many funeral service providers; however it may be better to get a personal insurance agent or see your Certified Financial Planner to arrange.

The manner in which a person can have their remains dealt with and the costs can leave family members in a difficult position in making decisions and agreeing.

As an estate planner I recommend you detail directions in a Funeral Memorandum (See **Funeral Instructions/Memorandum**), and provide them to your executor in advance of your Will.

Your 'Will as last resort' should detail your funeral arrangements that should be carried out if not already arranged. (I.e. cremation, burial, location, et cetera.)

- Earth burial is the usually the body being placed in a coffin or casket and buried in the ground in the traditional manor, covered in soil. Some people have skipped the coffin, and have been buried in just a shroud.
- Cremation is the burning or combustion of the body to ashes. Cremation is an alternative to burial and the ashes may be buried, interred or dispersed as per wishes.
- Body donation to science. Many medical schools accept anatomical donations; often cover the costs associated with retrieving the body, and returning cremated remains to the family.
- There are other choices. Some people want environmental options, others want more economical options, so you should make note of your customs, culture and beliefs related to your funeral and the processes you wish carried out.

Cremation has become a popular choice over the last half century or more as it can save money, and it can be simpler. You can have the body cremated and then spread the ashes over a place of choice or kept in an urn avoiding the cost of a casket and plot.

If you have decided to make an anatomical gift of your body to an institution, you should include instructions in case the donee declines for some unknown reason. You should also include your instructions for a ritual or memorial service.

Memorial societies exist in many jurisdictions to help find simpler and cheaper options in an increasingly expensive funeral services market. They help members plan and arrange for funeral or cremation without the pressure of providing an extravagant funeral.

Do it yourself options do exist in many jurisdictions. You can buy your own casket or even a shroud, have a family member arrange to receive and transport the body, get death certificates or permits, deliver to a crematorium or burial plot, and arrange a private memorial service. It is wise to get estimates on all options.

Some costs and considerations associated with burial decision;
- Transportation of the body from place to place
- Casket
- Embalming and/or cosmetic restoration and services by funeral home
- Vault or Grave liner
- Viewing service and facility
- Ritual service
- Grave plot
- Open and closing grave
- Transportation of mourners
- Clergy fee
- Obituary fees
- Copies of death certificate
- Music
- Flowers

Some costs and considerations associated with cremation decision;
- Transportation of the body from place to place
- Viewing service and facility
- Casket for service
- Crematorium charges and container
- Urn and and/or plot (Columbarium)
- Ritual service

- Transportation of mourners
- Clergy fee
- Obituary fees
- Copies of death certificate
- Music
- Flowers

It is often recommended that funeral arrangements be left in memorandum form so they can easily be accessed before the Will is read.

You can fill in our detailed section on funeral instructions, then sign it, let your executor or family know where it is, and have your lawyer review if you wish to make it legal.

It is wise to review the funeral and burial laws of your jurisdiction while planning. There are often laws and regulations related to who can or will be responsible for your funeral and burial, where you can be buried, where ashes can be spread, whether embalming is required, and dealing with funeral homes and mortuary contracts.

e) Body or Organ Donation

Make your wishes known on how you feel about body or organ donation.

There are many reasons to donate your body or organs. Everyone should consider themselves potential donor no matter your age or medical history. Even if your organs can't be used, it's likely that you can be a tissue donor, giving anything from corneas to heart valves to a needy recipient. Your complete body can be donated to a university or medical school for research purposes or you can choose to donate only what you choose, for example, eye banks are one of the oldest organ donation options. So make sure to give organ donation serious thought.

Many possible body and organs that could be donated are not because potential donors didn't make their families aware of their wishes which lead to many people, who are waiting for an organ transplant, continuing to suffer or pass away.

If you're interested in donating your organs after you pass on, or if you want to make that decision for your family, there are steps you should take to ensure that it happens. Most jurisdictions have their own rules for body and/or organ donations so it's best to inform yourself of the rules. There are donor cards or a designation on your driver's license; you may contact a local university or medical school or you can also create a memorandum for organ or body donation so that it is available immediately.

While a signed donor card and a driver's license with an 'organ donor' designation are legal documents in most jurisdictions, it is during the window of opportunity i.e. in a hospital on a ventilator, that the next-of-kin will give the approval that you intended to be a donor. The timeline for organ donation is immediately after death.

So, it is very important that you discuss your wishes with your family and/or your executor/estate trustee beforehand, as the Will may not be read for days after death.

As organ donation can depend on the condition of your organs, body, et cetera, it is also advisable to indicate in the memorandum or in your funeral instructions (just in case) what is to be done if they are not accepted due to delay, an autopsy is required, poor condition, or other reason. The donee has the right to decline, and may not have the resources to deal with non-usable organ donations.

See '**APPENDIX – MEMORANDUMS**'

------

f) Conclusion

A Will is a very important and powerful document and you should think seriously about what you put into it. This book has explained most of the more common choices you can make, however, it is not all inclusive and the final decisions are yours and ultimately your responsibility.

There may be other items you may need to include in your Will or under a clause. Take note of any issue we may not have covered and discuss with your Certified Financial Planner and estate lawyer before completing.

We have provided a guide and workbook for you to understand many of the issues involved in writing your Will. You may use all in this book to write your own Will, and the final Will is your sole and full responsibility. We have indicated many times that you should seek other advice.

We recommend you complete the **APPENDIX - PERSONAL LEGACY WORKBOOK,** to help you get your wishes together, then complete the **WILL CLAUSE CHECKLIST** for the clauses you wish to use.

V.

APPENDIX - PERSONAL WORKBOOK:

GET YOUR WISHES ON PAPER

Fill in as much detail in each area with your wishes and notes. Refer back to the appropriate chapter when you need to review terms.

Cut out this section if you wish. Make a copy of this section for your spouse/partner, and also a working copy.

Any areas you are not ready to complete, skip and continue on, you may return to them later.

a) Estate Goals

Examples:

- Leave a neat and detailed estate
- Leave a suitable estate
- Provide for a dependent
- Minimize estate fees and tax
- Legacies or bequests
- Donate to charity
- Make your funeral wishes known
- Make your organ donation wishes

1) _____

2) _____

3) _____

4) _____

5) _____

6) _____

Additional notes on your estate wishes:

_____

_____

_____

_____

_____

b) Personal Information

- Fill in information on lines provided.

- Use margins for notes if necessary, as more detail is always constructive.

Your name

_____

Date of birth and place of birth

_____

Occupation

_____

Address

_____

Telephone (Home) (Work) (Mobile)

_____

Email

_____

Spouse, common-law or partner name

_____

Date of birth and place of birth

_____

Occupation

_____

Address

_____

Telephone (Home) (Work) (Mobile)

_____

Email

_____

Marital Status

Single   Yes __ No __

Married   Yes __ No __

Common-Law or partner (_____)   Yes __ No __

Divorced or separated   Yes __ No __

Previous - spouse, common-law or partner name

Name

_____

Date of birth and place of birth

_____

Jurisdiction of marriage

_____

Date of divorce   _____

Jurisdiction of divorce _____

Marriage or domestic contract?   Yes __ No __ (Provide copy)

Divorce, separation agreement or court order?   Yes __ No __ (Provide copy)

Your citizenship _____

Spouse/partner citizenship _____

Domicile or Permanent Home

_____

Previous marriage by either spouse   Yes __ No __

Whom? _____

Child support, alimony or other obligation?

_____

Location of any documents related to previous marriage, child support, alimony or any other obligation

_____

Children from current relationship:

Name   Date of birth

_____   _____

_____   _____

_____   _____

_____   _____

_____   _____

_____   _____

Children from a previous relationship:

Name   Date of birth

_____   _____

_____   _____

_____   _____

_____   _____

_____   _____

_____   _____

Are any children disabled?   Yes __ No __

Name   Nature of disability

_____   _____

_____   _____

_____   _____

_____   _____

_____   _____

_____   _____

Are there any other dependents?   Yes _____ No _____

Name   Relationship   Reason for dependence

_____ _____   _____

_____ _____   _____

_____ _____   _____

_____ _____   _____

_____ _____   _____

_____ _____   _____

Grandchildren:

Name   Date of birth

_____   _____

_____   _____

_____   _____

_____   _____

_____   _____

Parents (Indicate if deceased) Name(s)

_____

Phone Number(s)

_____

Address(s)

_____

Parents of spouse (Indicate if deceased)

Name(s)

_____

Phone Number(s)

_____

Address(s)

_____

Location of any documents related to dependents

_____

Notes:

_____

_____

c) Medical Information

Personal Physician Name

_____

Phone Number

_____

Address

_____

Spouse, common-law or partner Personal Physician Name

_____

Phone Number

Address

_____

Location of any documents related to above information

_____

Specialist Physician Name (s)

_____

Phone Number

_____

Address

_____

Spouse, common-law or partner Personal Physician Name

_____

Phone Number

_____

Address

_____

d) Property and Financial Information

i) Income information

Current annual income

Employment	_____	Business	_____
Rent	_____	Royalties	_____
Pension	_____	Other	_____
Other	_____	Other	_____

Notes on income sources: (i.e. Pension, business, rental details)

_____

_____

_____

_____

_____

ii) Asset Information

1.   Real Estate Properties (location and value)

Home

_____

Is this a Matrimonial Home?   Yes _____   No _____

Cottage

_____

Investment property

_____

Foreign property

_____

In whose name is the real estate if other than you?

_____

_____

2.   Personal Use Property: (Approximate Value)

Valuables such as jewelry, paintings, heirlooms, china, gold, silver, coins, china, memorabilia, etc.

Item name   Approximate Value

_____   _____

_____   _____

_____   _____

_____   _____

_____   _____

_____   _____

_____   _____

Personal use items not listed above (i.e. vehicles, boat, ATV, cabin, land?)

                         Approximate Value

     Automobile   _____

Automobile	_____
Boat	_____
ATV	_____
Cabin	_____
Land	_____
Other	_____
Other	_____

Household goods -   Approximate Value

Furniture	_____
Machinery	_____
Tools	_____
Equipment	_____

3. Financial Institution(s) Accounts (Savings, checking, safety deposit.)

Financial Institution(s) name & address _____

Account Holder(s) _____   _____

Financial Institution(s) name & address _____

Account Holder(s) _____   _____

Safety deposit box (location and in whose name?)

Financial Institution(s) name & address _____

Account Holder(s) _____   _____

If you have more than one financial institution, please copy these pages.

4. Individual Non-Registered Investment Assets

Financial Institution(s) name & address

_____

Type	Market Value	Adjusted Cost Base
Stocks	$ _____	_____
Bonds	$ _____	_____
ETFs	$ _____	_____
Mutual Funds	$ _____	_____
GICs	$ _____	_____

Bank Accounts $ _____ _____

Cryptocurrency $ _____ _____

Other _____ $ _____ _____

Other _____ $ _____ _____

Other _____ $ _____ _____

5. Joint Non-Registered Investment Assets

Financial Institution(s) name & address _____

Type	Market Value	Adjusted Cost Base
Stocks	$ _____	_____
Bonds	$ _____	_____
ETFs	$ _____	_____
Mutual Funds	$ _____	_____
GICs	$ _____	_____
Bank Accounts	$ _____	_____
Cryptocurrency	$ _____	_____
Other _____	$ _____	_____
Other _____	$ _____	_____
Other _____	$ _____	_____

6. Retirement, Pension or Registered Investment Accounts

   (RPP, RRSP, Education Plan, 401K, etc.)

Financial Institution(s) name & address _____

Type	Face Value	Beneficiary (s)	Account held with
_____	$_____	_____	_____
_____	$_____	_____	_____
_____	$_____	_____	_____
_____	$_____	_____	_____
_____	$_____	_____	_____
_____	$_____	_____	_____
_____	$_____	_____	_____

_____ $_____ _____ _____
_____ $_____ _____ _____
_____ $_____ _____ _____

7. Business Ownership Interests

Company name   Ownership percentage

_____   _____

_____   _____

8. Life Insurance Policies

Policy number Type of coverage   Beneficiary (s) Insurance Company
               (Term 10, UL, etc.)   (Named on policy)

_____ _____ _____ _____

_____ _____ _____ _____

_____ _____ _____ _____

_____ _____ _____ _____

_____ _____ _____ _____

_____ _____ _____ _____

Location of policies

_____

_____

9. Debts Owing to You by a Third Party

Name   Details

_____   _____

_____   _____

_____   _____

_____   _____

10. Inheritance

(To Come? From whom, from where, relationship, amount?)

_____

_____

_____

_____

Location of any documents related to above assets

_____

_____

_____

_____

vii) Liabilities

Mortgages

_____   _____

_____   _____

_____   _____

_____   _____

Loans, credit card balances, other debts.

Type	Amount	Holder of debt (Financial Institution)

Location of any documents related to above liabilities

_____

_____

_____

_____

viii) Other Items of Note: (Location, number, details)

Safety deposit box key,

_____

Post office box key/number

_____

Other keys

_____

Combination locks

_____

Safe combination

_____

Hiding place for items

_____

Burglar alarm code(s)

_____

Copyrights, patents, trademarks

_____

Tax records are held

_____

Court judgement pending

_____

Additional notes on any of the above items of note:

_____

_____

_____

_____

_____

_____

_____

e) Digital Account Information

Attention: This section's details especially should be kept in a very safe place. i.e. Safe or safety deposit box.

Devices, email, internet accounts, accounts/cards and memberships – Identification (ID), passwords, PINs, etc. (Fill in as much as known.)

Digital devices – i.e. phone, desktop, laptop, notebook.

Device _____

      User ID _____ Password _____

Device _____

      User ID _____ Password _____

Device _____

      User ID _____ Password _____

Device _____

      User ID _____ Password _____

Mobile Device 1 _____

      User ID _____ Password _____

      Voicemail: _____

Mobile Device 2 _____

      User ID _____ Password _____

      Voicemail: _____

Virtual Private Network (VPN) -   Name _____

      User ID _____ Password _____

Locked files or folders -   Name _____

      User ID _____ Password _____

Disk or file encryption details

_____

_____

Email accounts

Email 1- Provider (i.e. hotmail.com) _____

      User ID _____ Password _____

Email 2- Provider (i.e. hotmail.com) _____

       User ID _____ Password _____

Internet accounts

Facebook

       User ID _____ Password _____

LinkedIn

       User ID _____ Password _____

Twitter

       User ID _____ Password _____

MySpace

       User ID _____ Password _____

Instagram _____

       User ID _____ Password _____

Other _____

       User ID _____ Password _____

Other _____

       User ID _____ Password _____

Other _____

       User ID _____ Password _____

Codes, passwords and PIN numbers

ATM card 1   _____

ATM card 2   _____

ATM card 3   _____

Garage door   _____

Credit card   _____

Credit card   _____

Alarm system   _____

On-line trading   _____

Other   _____

Other   _____

Other   _____

Other   _____

Other   _____

Do you use password management software?   Yes ___ No ___

  Details: _____

Location of any documents related to above information

_____

Other items of note:

_____

_____

_____

_____

f)   Professional and Personal Contacts

Certified Financial Planner/Broker/Advisor - Name

_____

Phone Numbers _____

Address

_____

Lawyer – Name

_____

Phone Numbers _____

Address

_____

Personal Banker/ Name

_____

Phone Numbers _____

Address

_____

Employee Benefits Representative - Name

_____

Phone Numbers _____

Address

_____

Insurance Agent/Auto/Home/Marine/Umbrella - Name

_____

Phone Numbers _____

Address

_____

Insurance Agent/Auto/Home/Marine/Umbrella - Name

_____

Phone Numbers _____

Address

_____

Next of kin - Name _____

Phone Numbers _____

Address

_____

Clergy Name

_____

Phone Numbers _____

Address

_____

Other - Name

_____

Phone Numbers _____

Address

_____

Other - Name

_____

Phone Numbers _____

Address

_____

Other - Name

_____

Phone Numbers _____

Address

_____

Other - Name

_____

Other - Name

_____

Other - Name

_____

Other - Name

_____

Other - Name

_____

Other - Name

_____

g) Instructions for Your Will

Where will you keep the original copy of your Will?

_____

Please refer back to 'Your Last Will and Testament' section as often as necessary to make sure you enter the correct information and add detail to the 'Notes' sections.

Do you revoke all previous Wills that were created before the date of the new Will?

Yes __ No __ Date of new Will? _____

i) Executor/Estate Trustee/Liquidator(s):

Name: _____ Relationship: _____

Name: _____ Relationship: _____

Address(es) of Executor/Estate Trustee/Liquidator (s):

_____

_____

ii) Alternate Executor/Estate Trustee/Liquidator(s)

(If initial predeceases you or is unable to act):

Name: _____ Relationship: _____

Name: _____ Relationship: _____

Address(es) of alternate Executor/Estate Trustee/Liquidator(s):

_____

_____

iii) Special Executor/Estate Trustee/Liquidator Provisions

(ie: Foreign Executor/Estate Trustee/Liquidator for assets in another jurisdiction?)

_____

iv) Powers for the Executor et al

Powers for the executor/estate trustee/trustee, liquidator or personal representative(s) to manage assets.

Give careful consideration to these powers to allow the trustees to act flexibly in administering the trust assets. (See **'Powers'** in Trusts section.)

- Investments   Yes __ No __
- Payments from trusts   Yes __ No __
- To sell and/or retain assets   Yes __ No __
- Borrow or lend money   Yes __ No __
- Renew or maintain debt obligations   Yes __ No __
- Retain and/or employ agents and advisors   Yes __ No __

v) Executor/Estate Trustee et al Compensation   Yes __ No __

'Gift' or a specific fee or percentage.

_____

_____

_____

_____

vi) Bequests

(i.e.: jewelry, art, individual personal items or articles, family heirlooms):

You can choose to create a Personal Property Memorandum instead with a detailed list of items and for whom. If you wish to do this see Personal Property memorandum at the end. Refer to it in your Will.

If you have only a few specific bequests, list them here.

Please list your specific bequests

Name: _____

Bequest: _____

Name: _____

Bequest: _____

Name: _____

Bequest: _____

Name: _____

Bequest: _____

Name: _____

Bequest: _____

Name: _____

Bequest: _____

Name: _____

Bequest: _____

Name: _____

Bequest: _____

Name: _____

Bequest: _____

vii) Cash Legacies:

You may leave specific cash amounts to people or charities in your Will provided there will be cash available in the estate after-taxes.

Name: _____

Legacy: _____

Name: _____

Legacy: _____

Name: _____

Legacy: _____

Name: _____

Legacy: _____

Name: _____

Legacy: _____

viii) Exclusion(s)

Explain why a person or persons were excluded from the Will. It can reduce the possibility of arguments later.

Name: _____

Explanation: _____

_____

_____

Name: _____

Explanation: _____

_____

_____

ix) Estate Residue:

Distribution of Estate Residue after bequests and legacies are complete:

Primary beneficiary(s) – please indicate relationship (i.e. spouse, father, mother, sister, brother, etc.)

Name: _____   Relationship: _____

Name: _____   Relationship: _____

Name: _____   Relationship: _____

Name: _____   Relationship: _____

Name: _____   Relationship: _____

Name: _____   Relationship: _____

If spouse and/or children and a trust(s) to be created.

Provisions for a Spouse ((including financial support, and when spouse will receive income, capital, and/or full distribution from any trust)?):

Notes:

_____

_____

_____

_____

Trustee(s):

Name: _____ Relationship: _____

Name: _____ Relationship: _____

Name: _____ Relationship: _____

Provisions for Children (including financial support, and ages at which they receive income, capital, and/or full distribution from trust):

Notes:

_____

_____

_____

_____

Trustee(s):

Name: _____ Relationship: _____

Name: _____ Relationship: _____

Name: _____ Relationship: _____

x) Powers for the Trustee(s)

(Trust Name 1 _____)

Give careful consideration to these powers to allow the trustees to act flexibly in administering the trust assets. (See **'Powers'** in Trusts section.)

- Investments   Yes __ No __
- Payments from trusts   Yes __ No __
- To sell and/or retain assets   Yes __ No __
- Borrow or lend money   Yes __ No __
- Renew or maintain debt obligations   Yes __ No __

- Entitlement to compensation   Yes __ No __
- Retain and/or employ agents and advisors   Yes __ No __
- Other: _____

Powers for the Trustee(s)

(Trust Name 2 _____)

Give careful consideration to these powers to allow the trustees to act flexibly in administering the trust assets. (See **'Powers'** in Trusts section.)

- Investments   Yes __ No __
- Payments from trusts   Yes __ No __
- To sell and/or retain assets   Yes __ No __
- Borrow or lend money   Yes __ No __
- Renew or maintain debt obligations   Yes __ No __
- Entitlement to compensation   Yes __ No __
- Retain and/or employ agents and advisors   Yes __ No __

Other: _____

Alternate beneficiary(s) **Failure or Common Disaster** - if none of above beneficiaries are alive or if all die in common accident:

Name: _____   Relationship: _____

Name: _____   Relationship: _____

Special instructions: (i.e. Number of days you predecease person)

_____

_____

Trustee(s):

Name: _____   Relationship: _____

Name: _____   Relationship: _____

Powers for the Trustee(s)

(Trust Name 3 _____)

Give careful consideration to these powers to allow the trustees to act flexibly in administering the trust assets. (See **'Powers'** in Trusts section.)

- Investments   Yes __ No __
- Payments from trusts   Yes __ No __
- To sell and/or retain assets   Yes __ No __
- Borrow or lend money   Y   es __ No __
- Renew or maintain debt obligations   Yes __ No __
- Entitlement to compensation   Yes __ No __
- Retain and/or employ agents and advisors   Yes __ No __
- Other: _____

Divorce - related to beneficiaries: (Separate property?)
Notes:

_____

_____

_____

Children outside of wedlock:
Notes:

_____

_____

_____

_____

xi) Guardianship:

Guardian(s):

Name   Relationship

_____   _____

_____   _____

Address(es) of Guardian(s):

_____

_____

Alternate Guardian(s):

Name   Relationship

_____   _____

_____   _____

Address(es) of alternate Guardian(s):

_____

_____

Special Guardian Provisions: (Notes on health care matters such as medical treatments, religious beliefs, cultural preferences, compensation or other items that provide more relative guidance for your guardian in future decision making.)

_____

_____

_____

_____

_____

_____

_____

_____

_____

_____

xii) Will for Assets in Another Jurisdiction

It is important to have a separate Will for assets in other jurisdictions, made in that jurisdiction.

Do you have assets in another state, province or country?   Yes ___ No ___

Do you have a separate Will for these assets?   Yes ___ No ___

VI.

APPENDIX - MEMORANDUMS

Tangible Personal Property Memorandum

Bequests

(i.e.: jewelry, art, individual personal items or articles, family heirlooms):

Please list your specific bequests

Name: _____

Bequest: _____

Name: _____

Bequest: _____

Name: _____

Bequest: _____

Name: _____

Bequest: _____

Name: _____

Bequest: _____

Name: _____

Bequest: _____

I expressly adjoin by reference this memorandum into my Will.

Signature: _____ **Date:** _____

Funeral Instructions/Memorandum

It is a good practice to get information on funeral options and costs associated.

Cost and consideration estimates associated with burial decision: (From your research)

- Transportation of the body from place to place _____
- Casket _____
- Embalming or cosmetic restoration and services by funeral home _____
- Vault or Grave liner _____
- Viewing service and facility _____
- Ritual service _____
- Grave plot _____
- Open and closing grave _____
- Transportation of mourners _____
- Clergy fee _____
- Obituary fees _____
- Copies of death certificate _____
- Music _____
- Flowers _____

Cost and consideration estimates associated with cremation decision:

- Transportation of the body from place to place _____
- Viewing service and facility _____
- Casket for service _____
- Crematorium charges and container _____
- Urn and plot (Columbarium) _____
- Ritual service _____
- Transportation of mourners _____
- Clergy fee _____
- Obituary fees _____
- Copies of death certificate _____
- Music _____
- Flowers _____

How will your funeral be paid for? (i.e. funds from estate, insurance policy, prepaid details, et cetera.)

_____

_____

My thoughts as to my funeral related to customs, culture and beliefs, traditional funeral or an informal gathering:

_____

_____

Have you made funeral arrangements? Yes ____ No ____

Funeral Provider Name _____

Phone Number _____

Address _____

_____

Do you own a cemetery plot and have you arranged for ongoing care and maintenance?

Yes__ No__

_____

_____

Have you prepaid for your funeral? Yes ____ No ____

_____

_____

If you have not made arrangements:

Do you wish to be cremated or buried? Cremated _____ Burial _____

Earth burial, mausoleum entombment, cremation, inurnment, internment, grave, crypt, niche, other details?

_____

_____

Are instructions in your Will or elsewhere? Yes ____ No ____

If yes, location:

_____

Visitation: (Funeral home, church, home, other)

_____

_____

Preferred or suggested funeral or cremation service provider,

_____

_____

Location:

_____

_____

Transfer service, (If not to be provided by above service provider.)

_____

_____

Cemetery,

_____

_____

Location:

_____

_____

Clergy,

_____

_____

Cremated:

Type of urn:

_____

_____

Instructions for service,

_____

_____

_____

_____

_____

Buried:

Type of casket:

_____

_____

Open or closed casket? Open _____ Closed _____

Instructions for service, (In addition to all below)

_____

_____

_____

_____

_____

_____

Memorial service: (Instructions in addition to below, if body is donated, not present, et cetera.)

_____

_____

Headstone or monument:

_____

_____

Inscription/epitaph for headstone, or monument:

_____

_____

Music selection for funeral and service:

_____

_____

_____

_____

Readings at funeral and service: (Hymns/Scriptures, poem, et cetera.)

_____

_____

_____

_____

Floral requests or donations in lieu of flowers?

_____

_____

_____

_____

Clothing and dressing requests:

_____

_____

_____

_____

Jewelry requests:

_____

_____

Jewelry to be returned after service to estate trustee/executor to follow Will instructions?

_____

_____

Glasses On _____ Off _____

To be buried with you: Jewelry listed _____ Glasses _____

Items to be displayed: awards, trophies, crafts, specific photos, et cetera.

_____

_____

Organizations you would like notified: Company, school, troupe, band, lodge, society or fraternal organization

_____

_____

_____

_____

Notes or details to add to obituary: (Besides below)

_____

_____

_____

_____

_____

_____

Obituary to be published in the following:

_____

_____

Place of birth

_____

Date of birth _____

Married _____

Wedding date _____

Religious affiliation

_____

Clubs, lodges, et cetera.

_____

Military service / war record

_____

Information about employment

_____

_____

Spouse, widow or widower of

_____

Date of death of spouse

_____

Children and residence

_____

_____

_____

_____

Grandchildren and residence

_____

_____

_____

_____

Siblings and residence

_____

_____

_____

_____

Pall Bearer's Names:

_____

_____

_____

_____

_____

_____

_____

Honorary Pall Bearer's

_____

_____

_____

_____

_____

_____

_____

Other notes related to wishes, beliefs, processes, rituals, culture, details, et cetera.:

_____

_____

_____

_____

_____

_____

_____

_____

_____

_____

_____

I expressly adjoin by reference this memorandum into my Will.

Signature: _____ **Date:** _____

Body or Organ Donation Memorandum

I wish to include the following wishes and/or have them be known in a memorandum.

I would like to donate:

Full body   Yes _____   No _____

All organs   Yes _____   No _____

Other detailed below: Yes _____   No _____

Notes:

_____

_____

If you wish to express in more detail your wishes related to your choice above.

i.e. Full body to a university or medical research institution

i.e. Only these organs, heart, lungs, liver, et cetera.

i.e. Only my eyes to an eye bank

i.e. All organs but not remaining tissue

_____

_____

_____

_____

_____

_____

_____

_____

I expressly adjoin by reference this memorandum into my Will.

Signature: _____ **Date:** _____

VII.

WILL CLAUSE CHECKLIST

[Example 1.1 (Introductory Clause/Exordium Clause)

[Example 1.2 (Introductory Clause/Exordium Clause)

[Example 1.3 (Introductory Clause/Exordium Clause)

[Example 1.4 (Introductory Clause/Exordium Clause in Contemplation of Marriage)

[Example 2.1 (Revocation Clause)

[Example 2.2 (Revocation Clause)

[Example 2.3 (Revocation Clause)

[Example 3.1 (Defining and/or Gender Clause)

[Example 3.2 (Defining and/or Gender Clause)

[Example 4.1 (Appoint an executor/estate representative clause)

[Example 4.2 (Appoint an executor/estate representative clause)

[Example 4.3 (One executor with alternate.)

[Example 4.4 (Two executors acting jointly, with alternate, with sole successor executor.)

[Example 4.5 (Giving one executor veto or decision making authority)

[Example 4.6 (Exclusion of a person from acting as an executor clause)

[Example 5.1 (Waiver to Post Bond or to a Surety Clause)

[Example 5.2 (Waiver to Post Bond or to a Surety Clause)

[Example 6.1 (Vesting/transfer of property to the executor clause)

[Example 6.3 (Vesting/transfer of property to the executor clause)

[Example 6.4 (Vesting/transfer of property to the executor clause)

[Example 6.5 (Executor Trusts: Vesting/transfer of property to the executor clause)

[Example 6.6 (Executor Trusts: Vesting/transfer of property to the executor clause)

[Example 7.1 (Debts, taxes and testamentary expenses clause)

[Example 7.2 (Debts, taxes and testamentary expenses clause)

[Example 7.3 (Debts, taxes and testamentary expenses clause)

[Example 7.4 (Debts, taxes and testamentary expenses clause)

[Example 8.1 (Residue Clause)

[Example 8.2 (Residue Clause)

[Example 8.3 (Residue Clause)

[Example 8.4 (Residue Clause)

[Example 9.1 (Powers and fiduciary obligations of executor(s) clause)

[Example 10.1 (Naming Guardian(s))

[Example 10.2 (Naming Guardian(s))

[Example 11.1 (Simple clause for minors, without the need for a detailed testamentary trust)

[Example 11.2 (Simple clause for minors, to a guardian)

[Example 12.1 (Bequests)

[Example 12.2 (Bequests)

[Example 12.3 (Bequests)

[Example 12.4 (Legacies)

[Example 12.5 (Legacies)

[Example 12.6 (Legacies)

[Example 12.7 (Legacies)

[Example 12.8 (Devise(s)

[Example 12.9 (Devise(s) Add-ons: (For mortgages, debts, or taxes))

[Example 12.10 (Devise(s) Add-ons: (For mortgages, debts, or taxes))

[Example 13.1 (Appointing a Trustee or Trustees, single trustee)

[Example 13.2 (Appointing a Trustee or Trustees, two trustees with one having veto)

[Example 13.3 (Excluding someone as a trustee)

[Example 13.4 (Trust for minor with executor and another trustee.)

[Example 13.5 (Trust for minor with executors previously appointed (executors are trustees).)

[Example 13.6 (Trust for minors with executor and another trustee.)

[Example 13.7 (Trust for minors with executor(s).)

[Example 13.8 (Insurance Trust for minors with one trustee.)

[Example 13.9 (Life interest trust clause for a common law spouse.)

[Example 13.10 (Powers for Trustee(s) and/or Executor(s))

[Example 13.11 (Powers for Trustee(s) and/or Executor(s))

[Example 14.1 (Common disaster with survival)

[Example 14.2 (Failure)

[Example 14.3 (Gift Over)

[Example 15.1 (Divorce and community/family property clause)

[Example 16.1 (Exclusion of a person from your Will)

[Example 17.1 (Testimonial and Attestation Clauses/ Signature, and Witnesses to the Will)

[Example 17.2 (Testimonial and Attestation Clauses/ Signature, and Witnesses to the Will)

[Example 17.3 (Testimonial and Attestation Clauses/ Signature, and Witnesses to the Will)

[Example 18.1 (Codicil)

[Example 19.1 (Memorandum)

Best practice/recommendations for writing your Will are:

- Refer back to the examples in the book as you make your checklist.
- There are many ways to copy clauses from the page into a word processing document. For example with Google Drive you can scan or take a picture of the clause, then upload and copy/paste/edit in a document to create your Will.

To order a copy of any and all clauses, you can check off your chosen clauses and email this as an order form to estategta@gmail.com.

The administration fee for most clauses is $5 per clause. More comprehensive clauses are $10 each, such as Powers of the Executor(s) and Trustee(s). Send this form with your clearly checked clauses, we will send you a quote and payment details to be completed in advance of sending the document with the clauses.

We plan to have a website with these options and others by the 2nd edition.

Full Name: _____

Your Email: _____

VIII.

WILL TEMPLATES/EXAMPLES

<u>Disclaimer:</u> We are not making recommendations on the use of these templates; our objective has been to provide information to help you write your own Will. Years of experience in Estate Planning, Management and Administration, plus years of reading and research has allowed us to provide this publication, however, given the differences in jurisdictional rules the choice to use these for your personal situation is yours alone and you must bear all responsibility in using any and all in this publication to write your own Will.

A properly executed Will in most jurisdictions has the testator declare to the witnesses that they are about to see him/her sign their Last Will and Testament at the end of the document, and he/she the testator then signs the document. The witnesses then sign a short declaration in the Will that they were present and witnessed the testator's signature. A good practice is for the testator to begin by initialing each page of the Will in succession, each witness initial each page with the testator, then complete with the testator's signature and witness signatures as mentioned in the appropriate areas.

1) **Simple Will:** The first Will Template is a very basic, simple Will. It may be considered for those who:
   - Have very little assets to pass on.
   - Will pass on to one person.
   - Need to complete quickly.

It contains the following clauses:

1. Introductory Clause/Exordium Clause
2. Revocation Clause
3. Appoint an executor/estate representative clause
4. Residue Clause)with(Debts, taxes and testamentary expenses clause
5. Testimonial and Attestation Clauses/ Signature, and Witnesses to the Will

LAST WILL AND TESTAMENT

This is the Last Will and Testament of _____, of
_____, made this _____ day of _____, _____.

I revoke all my prior wills and codicils.

I appoint as my executor my _____, _____.

I give all of my property to my _____, _____, after my debts, funeral and testamentary
expenses are paid.

Signed by the testator in our joint presence and attested by us in the presence of him/her and of each other,

Testator Signature _____

1ˢᵗ Witness Signature _____

2ⁿᵈ Witness Signature _____

2) Individual or couple with mirror Wills

This template/example can be considered by an individual, or a couple making mirror Wills.

It contains the following clauses:

1. Introductory/exordium clause with revocation clause
2. Defining and/or gender clause
3. Appoint an executor/estate representative clause.
4. Waiver to post bond or to a Surety clause
5. Vesting/transfer of property to the executor clause
6. Debts, taxes and testamentary expenses clause
7. Powers and fiduciary obligations of executor(s) clause
8. Residue Clause
9. Failure Clause
10. Testimonial and attestation clauses with signature, and witnesses to the Will

LAST WILL AND TESTAMENT

I, _____, resident in the , City/Town of _____, in the Province/Territory/State of _____, in the Country of _____, being of sound mind, having sound and effective memory, not acting under duress or undue influence, and fully understanding the nature and extent of all my property and the disposition of said property, do hereby make, publish, and declare this document to be my Last Will and Testament, (From here on referred to as my Will), and do hereby revoke any and all other wills and codicils previously made by me, _____, made this _____ day of _____, _____.

Words used in this my Will regardless of the gender or number specifically used, shall be deemed and construed to include any other gender, masculine, feminine or neuter, or the singular and plural as the context requires.

I appoint my, _____, _____ to serve as the sole Executor/Executrix of this my Will, and I herein after refer to him/her as my 'Executor'. If he/she is unwilling or unable to act as my Executor, I appoint my, _____, _____ as sole Executor of this my Will.

I declare that my named executor, co-executor or alternate, who is not resident in _____, shall not be required to post a bond and/or security for acting as my executor.

I give, devise and bequeath all my property of every nature and kind and wherever situate, including any property over which I may have a general power of appointment, to my said Executor upon the following trusts, namely:

I direct my executor to pay from the capital of my estate, my enforceable debts, my funeral expenses, my testamentary expenses, my income taxes, and all my estate, legacy, succession or inheritance duties and/or taxes imposed pursuant to the laws of any jurisdiction in connection with any of my property, my accounts or my contracts upon my death.

My executor is given all of the powers deemed necessary to administer the estate, including all powers granted under this jurisdiction's law, subject to the executor's fiduciary duties to the beneficiaries and any restrictions or limits set forth under this jurisdiction's law. The powers of the executor include, but are not limited to:

i. Collect, manage, and invest estate assets, the accumulation and distribution of income and principal, in any form of property in which a prudent investor might invest;

ii. Borrow or lend money from the estate for estate purposes;

iii. Engage agents and professionals in their discretion to assist in the administration of the estate;

iv. Establish and administer any, bank, brokerage, other financial, and nonfinancial accounts for and on behalf of the estate;

v. Manage, operate, exercise obligations or sell any business that is an estate asset;

vi. Manage, sell, mortgage or lease any real or leasehold property that forms part of my estate;

vii. Deal with legal claims or actions concerning the estate or the assets and property in the estate;

viii. Prepare tax returns, make income tax elections and take any necessary or desirable actions with governmental agencies;

ix. My executor shall be fully exempt from any liability or loss to my estate due to any decision made under these powers in good faith. These powers do not include exoneration for fraud or gross negligence.

x. I hereby declare that each of my executors shall receive $_____ payable from the capital of the residue of my estate, as compensation for their acting as executors under this my Will.

I give, devise and bequeath the residue of my estate, both real and personal, of every nature and kind and wheresoever situate, including any property over which I may have a general power of appointment, to my _____, _____, if he/she survives me for a period of thirty (30) days, for his/her, own use absolutely.

If any part of my estate should fail to vest, my trustee shall give this share to be divided in equal shares per stirpes amongst his/her/their descendants who survive him/her/them provided they are living at the final distribution date. If this fails it should be given to my next of kin.

I hereby sign my name to this my Last Will and Testament, written on these ____ pages of paper, this _____ day of _____, 20__.

Signed, Published and Declared,

By the said Testator, _____,

(Print Full Name)

_____

(Testator Signature)

The foregoing instrument was signed, and declared by _____, the above-named Testator to be such Testator's Last Will and Testament in our presence, all being present at the same time, and we, at such Testator's request and in such Testator's presence and in the presence of each other, have subscribed our names as witnesses on the date above written.

_____, _____

Print Witness Name (1)   Address 1

_____,

Witness Signature

_____, _____

Print Witness Name (2)   Address 1

_____,

Witness Signature

3) Couple making mirror Wills, who have minor children.

This template/example can be used by a couple making mirror Wills, who have minor children.

It can include these clauses:

1) Introductory/exordium clause with revocation clause
2) Defining and/or gender clause
3) Appoint an executor with alternate.
4) Giving one executor veto or decision making authority
5) Waiver to post bond or to a Surety clause
6) Vesting/transfer of property to the executor clause
7) Debts, taxes and testamentary expenses
8) Residue Clause
9) Naming Guardian(s)
10) Trust for minors with executor(s) as trustees
11) Powers and fiduciary obligations of executor(s) clause
12) Failure Clause
13) Testimonial and attestation clauses with signature, and witnesses to the Will

Last Will and Testament

I, _____, resident in the , City/Town of _____, in the Province/Territory/State of _____, in the Country of _____, being of sound mind, having sound and effective memory, not acting under duress or undue influence, and fully understanding the nature and extent of all my property and the disposition of said property, do hereby make, publish, and declare this document to be my Last Will and Testament, (From here on referred to as my Will), and do hereby revoke any and all other wills and codicils previously made by me, _____, made this _____ day of _____, _____.

Words used in this my Will regardless of the gender or number specifically used, shall be deemed and construed to include any other gender, masculine, feminine or neuter, or the singular and plural as the context requires.

I appoint my [relationship - husband/wife/common law spouse/son/daughter/friend/lawyer, et cetera.], _____ and my [relationship - husband/wife/common law spouse/son/daughter/friend/lawyer, et cetera.], _____ to serve as Co-Executors/Executrixes of this my Will, and I herein after refer to him/her as my executor and/or trustee. If either of them is unable or unwilling to serve, the remaining Executor shall continue to serve as sole successor Executor hereunder. If both of these Executors of this my Will are unwilling or unable to serve, I appoint my [relationship - husband/wife/common law spouse/son/daughter/friend/lawyer, et cetera.], _____ sole Executor of this my Will.

I declare that my named executor, co-executor or alternate, who is not resident in _____, shall not be required to post a bond and/or security for acting as my executor.

I request that my executors make every reasonable effort to make their decisions jointly and unanimously, however, in the event they are unable to do so, _____ shall have the ultimate decision making authority.

I give, devise and bequeath all my property of every nature and kind and wherever situate, including any property over which I may have a general power of appointment, to my said Executor upon the following trusts, namely:
I direct my executor to pay from the capital of my estate, my enforceable debts, my funeral expenses, my testamentary expenses, my income taxes, and all my estate, legacy, succession or inheritance duties and/or taxes imposed pursuant to the laws of any jurisdiction in connection with any of my property, my accounts or my contracts upon my death.

I leave the residue of my estate to my [relationship - husband/wife/common law spouse/son/daughter/friend/lawyer, et cetera.],_____ if living on the 30th day following my death.

If my [relationship - husband/wife/common law spouse,], predeceases me, I appoint my [relationship – uncle/aunt/cousin/son/daughter/friend/lawyer, et cetera.], _____, *[relationship – uncle/ aunt/ cousin/ son/ daughter/ friend/ lawyer, et cetera.],*

_____ *as guardians of my minor children. If for any reason they cannot act as guardian, I appoint my [relationship – uncle/ aunt/ cousin/ son/ daughter/ friend/ lawyer, et cetera.],*

_____ *as guardian of my minor children. Any person named as a guardian or custodian is not required to post any security or bond.*

If my [relationship - husband/ wife/ common law spouse,], predeceases me, all property left in this my Will, to my children, _____,

_____*, and shall be held in trust for him/ her. Upon my children attaining the age of 25 years, such share or the amount then remaining shall be paid or transferred to him/ her.*

My trustee shall set aside each share as a separate trust and shall keep such share invested and, may from time to time until he/ she becomes absolutely entitled to all the capital, pay to or apply the benefit to the beneficiary, any of the income and the capital or part of, as my Trustee in his absolute discretion deem advisable from time to time remaining in trust.

My executors and/ or trustees is given all of the powers deemed necessary to administer the estate and any trusts created, including all powers granted under this jurisdiction's law, subject to the executor's fiduciary duties to the beneficiaries and any restrictions or limits set forth under this jurisdiction's law. The powers of the executor include, but are not limited to:

   i.   *Collect, manage, and invest estate assets, the accumulation and distribution of income and principal, in any form of property in which a prudent investor might invest;*

   ii.   *Borrow or lend money from the estate for estate purposes;*

   iii.   *Engage agents and professionals in their discretion to assist in the administration of the estate;*

   iv.   *Establish and administer any, bank, brokerage, other financial, and nonfinancial accounts for and on behalf of the estate;*

   v.   *Manage, operate, exercise obligations or sell any business that is an estate asset;*

   vi.   *Manage, sell, mortgage or lease any real or leasehold property that forms part of my estate;*

   vii.   *Deal with legal claims or actions concerning the estate or the assets and property in the estate;*

   viii.   *Prepare tax returns, make income tax elections and take any necessary or desirable actions with governmental agencies;*

   ix.   *My executor shall be fully exempt from any liability or loss to my estate due to any decision made under these powers in good faith. These powers do not include exoneration for fraud or gross negligence.*

   x.   *I hereby declare that each of my executors shall receive $_____ payable from the capital of the residue of my estate, as compensation for their acting as executors under this my Will.*

If any part of my estate should fail to vest, my trustee shall give this share to be divided in equal shares per stirpes amongst his/ her/ their descendants who survive him/ her/ them provided they are living at the final distribution date. If this fails it should be given to my next of kin.

I hereby sign my name to this my Last Will and Testament, written on these ____ pages of paper, this _____ day of _____, 20__.

Signed, Published and Declared,
By the said Testator, _____ ,
(Print Full Name)

_____
(Testator Signature)

The foregoing instrument was signed, and declared by _____ , *the above-named*
Testator to be such Testator's Last Will and Testament in our presence, all being present at the same time,
and we, at such Testator's request and in such Testator's presence and in the presence of each other, have
subscribed our names as witnesses on the date above written.

_____ , _____
Print Witness Name (1)   *Address 1*
_____ ,
Witness Signature

_____ , _____
Print Witness Name (2)   *Address 1*
_____ ,
Witness Signature

4) Individual, or an older couple making mirror Wills (With PP Memorandum

This template/example can be considered by an individual, or an older couple making mirror Wills.

It contains the following clauses:

1) Introductory/exordium clause
2) Revocation clause
3) Defining and/or gender clause
4) Appoint an executor/estate representative clause.
5) Waiver to post bond or to a Surety clause
6) Vesting/transfer of property to the executor clause
7) Debts, taxes and testamentary expenses clause
8) Memorandum
9) Devise(s)
10) Powers and fiduciary obligations of executor(s) clause
11) Residue Clause
12) Failure Clause
13) Devise(s) Add-ons: For mortgages, debts, or taxes
14) Divorce and community/family property clause
15) Testimonial and attestation clauses with signature, and witnesses to the Will

LAST WILL AND TESTAMENT

I, being of sound mind and body do hereby declare that this document is the Last Will and Testament of 'First Name Middle Name Surname', of 'Permanent Residence and Jurisdiction', made this 'Date of Month' day of 'Month', 'Year', 'Occupation'.

I hereby revoke all former wills, codicils and testamentary dispositions of every nature and kind made previously.

Words used in this my Will regardless of the gender or number specifically used, shall be deemed and construed to include any other gender, masculine, feminine or neuter, or the singular and plural as the context requires.

I appoint my, _____, _____ to serve as the sole Executor/Executrix of this my Will, and I herein after refer to him/her as my 'Executor'. If he/she is unwilling or unable to act as my Executor, I appoint my, _____, _____ as sole Executor of this my Will.

I declare that my named executor, co-executor or alternate, who is not resident in _____, shall not be required to post a bond and/or security for acting as my executor.

I give, devise and bequeath all my property of every nature and kind and wherever situate, including any property over which I may have a general power of appointment, to my said executor upon the following trusts, namely:

I direct my executor to pay from the capital of my estate, my enforceable debts, my funeral expenses, my testamentary expenses, my income taxes, and all my estate, legacy, succession or inheritance duties and/or taxes imposed pursuant to the laws of any jurisdiction in connection with any of my property, my accounts or my contracts upon my death.

To my [relationship - husband/wife/common law spouse/son/daughter/friend/lawyer, et cetera.], _____ I devise and give my 'cabin' located at 'Address of Residence in Jurisdiction', provided (he/she) survives me, together with all furniture, appliances, dishes, silverware, art work; permanently maintained in the property, and tools necessary for the maintenance and operation of the property.

I may leave a Tangible Personal Property Memorandum apart from this my Will, gifting of some or all of my tangible personal property. If I do so and the memorandum can be adjoined by this reference in this my Will, or otherwise be legally binding, I direct that it be adjoined or followed and prevail over the disposition in this my Will. This provision shall apply whether the writing is executed before or after this my Will.

My executor is given all of the powers deemed necessary to administer the estate, including all powers granted under this jurisdiction's law, subject to the executor's fiduciary duties to the beneficiaries and any restrictions or limits set forth under this jurisdiction's law. The powers of the executor include, but are not limited to:

 i. *Collect, manage, and invest estate assets, the accumulation and distribution of income and principal, in any form of property in which a prudent investor might invest;*

 ii. *Borrow or lend money from the estate for estate purposes;*

 iii. *Engage agents and professionals in their discretion to assist in the administration of the estate;*

 iv. *Establish and administer any, bank, brokerage, other financial, and nonfinancial accounts for and on behalf of the estate;*

 v. *Manage, operate, exercise obligations or sell any business that is an estate asset;*

 vi. *Manage, sell, mortgage or lease any real or leasehold property that forms part of my estate;*

 vii. *Deal with legal claims or actions concerning the estate or the assets and property in the estate;*

viii.   *Prepare tax returns, make income tax elections and take any necessary or desirable actions with governmental agencies;*

ix.   *My executor shall be fully exempt from any liability or loss to my estate due to any decision made under these powers in good faith. These powers do not include exoneration for fraud or gross negligence.*

x.   *I hereby declare that each of my executors shall receive \$_____ payable from the capital of the residue of my estate, as compensation for their acting as executors under this my Will.*

I give, devise and bequeath the residue of my estate, both real and personal, of every nature and kind and wheresoever situate, including any property over which I may have a general power of appointment, to my _____, _____, if he/she survives me for a period of thirty (30) days, for his/her, own use absolutely.

If any part of my estate should fail to vest, my trustee shall give this share to be divided in equal shares per stirpes amongst his/her/their descendants who survive him/her/them provided they are living at the final distribution date. If this fails it should be given to my next of kin.

I declare that all property acquired by any beneficiary under my Will, shall be excluded from such beneficiary's community property, net family property, partnership, and shall not be subject to claims of ownership or division by such beneficiary's spouse or partner pursuant to legislation of any jurisdiction, it being my intention that all property together with the income from this property shall remain the separate property of a beneficiary named, free from all matrimonial rights or controls by his or her spouse.

All beneficiaries receiving specific property shall be responsible for any encumbrances such as mortgages, debts, or taxes on the transfer of ownership.

I hereby sign my name to this my Last Will and Testament, written on these ____ pages of paper, this _____ day of _____, 20__'.

Signed, Published and Delared,
By the said Testator, _____,
                                (Print Full Name)

_____
                         (Testator Signature)

The foregoing instrument was signed, and declared by _____, the above-named Testator to be such Testator's Last Will and Testament in our presence, all being present at the same time, and we, at such Testator's request and in such Testator's presence and in the presence of each other, have subscribed our names as witnesses on the date above written.

_____, _____

Print Witness Name (1)   *Address 1*

_____,

Witness Signature

_____, _____

Print Witness Name (2)   *Address 1*

_____,

Witness Signature

Tangible Personal Property Memorandum

Bequests

(i.e.: jewelry, art, individual personal items or articles, family heirlooms):

I bequeath my mother's wedding ring, to my [relationship - husband/wife/common law spouse/son/daughter/friend/lawyer, et cetera.], _____

I bequeath my guitar to my [relationship - husband/wife/common law spouse/son/daughter/friend/lawyer, et cetera.],
_____

I bequeath my car, _____, to my [relationship - husband/wife/common law spouse/son/daughter/friend/lawyer, et cetera.], _____

I bequeath all of my personal effects in my principal residence, together with all furniture, appliances, dishes, silverware, art work; permanently maintained in the property, and tools necessary for the maintenance and operation of the property, to my [relationship - husband/wife/common law spouse/son/daughter/friend/lawyer, et cetera.], _____

I expressly adjoin by reference this memorandum into my Will.

Signature: _____ **Date:** _____

IX.

AFFIDAVITS

AFFIDAVIT

In the Estate of _____, deceased

PROOF OF WILL

I, _____, of _____

in the State/Province of _____, make oath and say that on the _____day of

_____, _____, I was present and did see

_____, late of _____, in the State/Province of

_____, the Testa/tor/trix Will annexed, marked Exhibit 'A'; duly sign, publish and declare

the said Will, as and for his/her Last Will and Testament in my presence, and in the presence of

_____,the other subscribing witness thereto. That I and the said

_____,then and there signed our names to such Will as such witnesses, in the presence of

the said Testa/tor/trix, and that at the time of the said execution of the said Will the said Testa/tor/trix was of sound

and disposing mind, memory and understanding to the best of my belief.

SWORN at _____ ,

in the State/Province of _____ ,

on the _____ day of _____ ,_____ ,

before me.

_____   _____

Commissioner, Notary Public, Solicitor, etc.   Signature of Witness to Will

SELF-PROVING AFFIDAVIT

State of _____, in the county of _____

BEFORE ME, the undersigned authority, on this day personally appeared _____, _____, and _____, known to me to be the Testator and the witnesses, respectively, whose names are subscribed to the annexed or foregoing instrument in their respective capacities, and, all of said persons being by me duly sworn, the said _____, Testator, declared to me and to the said witnesses in my presence that said instrument is his or her Last Will and Testament, and that he or she had willingly made and executed it as his or her free act and deed; and the said witnesses, each on his or her oath stated to me, in the presence and hearing of the said Testator, that the said Testator had declared to them that said instrument is his or her Last Will and Testament, and that he or she executed same as such and wanted each of them to sign it as a witness; and upon their oaths each witness stated further that they did sign the same as witnesses in the presence of the said Testator and at his or her request; that he or she was at that time eighteen years of age or over and was of sound mind; and that each of said witnesses was then at least fourteen years of age.

_____
Testator

_____
Witness

_____
Witness

SWORN TO before me by the said _____, Testator, and by the said _____ and _____, Witnesses, this ____ day of _____ A.D. 20___.

_____
COMMISSIONER, NOTARY PUBLIC, SOLICITOR, ETC.

AFFIDAVIT OF EXECUTION OF WILL OR CODICIL

In the matter of the execution of a will or codicil of _____, deceased.

AFFIDAVIT

I, _____ of _____, _____
make oath and say/affirm:

1. On the _____ day of _____, _____, I was present and saw the document marked as Exhibit "A" to this affidavit executed by _____.

2. _____ executed the document in the presence of myself and _____ of _____, _____. We were both present at the same time, and signed the document in the testator's presence as attesting witnesses.

SWORN/AFFIRMED BEFORE me at

_____ ,

in the State/Province of

_____ ,   _____

on the _____ day of   Signature of Witness to Will

_____ ,_____ ,

before me.

_____
A Commissioner for Taking Affidavits *(or as may be)*

X.

WRITE YOUR OWN WILL:

Write your own Will:

Write in the clauses you choose, then use a word processor to type, print and get your witnesses.

_____

_____

_____

_____

_____

_____

_____

_____

_____

Made in the USA
Middletown, DE
27 December 2022